Letters to a Young Classroom Teacher

ALSO BY GERALD RISING

Program Your Calculator

Inside Your Calculator

Guidelines for Teaching School Mathematics (with Donovan Johnson)

The Nature Watch Collection Book One

The Nature Watch Collection Book Two

Birds and Birdwatching

Birder's Break

Letters to a Young Classroom Teacher

Gerald Rising

W. R. PARKS
www.WRParks.com

DEDICATION

To those wonderful young people who commit their careers to the future of our society by taking responsibility for the youth of our world, I dedicate this collection of letters.

Copyright © 2019 by Gerald Rising
All rights reserved.
ISBN 0-88493-054-8
Library of Congress Control Number: 2019936793
Published by William R. Parks www.wrparks.com

Letters to a Young Classroom Teacher
CONTENTS

Foreword 7
Acknowledgements 11
How to Read This Book 13

THE REAL WORLD

Letter One: My Own First Day 17
Letter Two: The Teaching Task 25
Letter Three: The School Environment 31
Letter Four: Before You Start 35
Letter Five: Discipline 39
Letter Six: Discrimination 51
Letter Seven: Textbooks and Curriculum Revision 55
Letter Eight: Organizing Instruction 61
Letter Nine: Classroom Testing 75
Letter Ten: Standardized Tests 81
Letter Eleven: Your Classroom 85
Letter Twelve: Technology 91

PERSONAL

Letter Thirteen: Your Teaching Subject 97
Letter Fourteen: Role Models 101
Letter Fifteen: A Personal Inventory 107
Letter Sixteen: Dealing with Disappointment 113

PEOPLE

Letter Seventeen: Students 121
Letter Eighteen: Individual Students 129
Letter Nineteen: Colleagues 141
Letter Twenty: Administrators 149

| Letter Twenty-one: Parents | 155 |

GOING FURTHER
Letter Twenty-two: A Bag of Tricks	163
Letter Twenty-three: Your Personal Reading	169
Letter Twenty-four: Professional Activities	173
Letter Twenty-five: The Possibility of Failure	179

ON YOUR WAY
| Letter Twenty-six: Ready, Set, Go | 189 |

APPENDICES
| My Background | 195 |
| Literature Cited | 199 |

Foreword

> *You are now about to peep behind the scenes of this teaching game*
> *and see the secret wires, pulleys, slap-sticks,*
> *and other annoying contraptions,*
> *which were never mentioned in your college courses.*
> —George Miller

The concept of this book is straightforward. I am recording in it the kinds of things I wish were discussed with me when I began teaching school English and mathematics classes. I am convinced that most of what I will have to say will apply every bit as much and possibly even more today than it did when I began classroom instruction of this important subject many years ago.

This is not a method, content or educational psychology textbook; rather, this book is meant to convey my suggestions to be considered at the time you young men and women take up your first teaching assignment and in the process cross the gulf between adolescence and adulthood.

I hope in fact that it will be a fast and entertaining read.

At the same time, I believe that the issues I raise and the opinions I offer are important. Entering a classroom and confronting a group of naïve students places major burdens on every teacher. The responsibility is great and I will be asking you to take that responsibility very seriously.

The idea of preparing these Letters came to me as I read E. O. Wilson's 2013 bestseller, *Letters to a Young Scientist,* and it is evident that I have modified his title for this book.

Wilson has written for young men and women who seek a career in scientific research and it is important for you to recognize the differences between research and teaching — as does Wilson. In fact, Wilson encourages prospective researchers to seek ways to *avoid* teaching. As a school classroom teacher, you are certainly a participant in the scientific endeavor, but you are not a participant in his more specific audience of scientific researchers. Anyone who reads both books will see clearly this distinction. I will return to this difference when I briefly address educational research in Letter Twenty-four.

But this book is not the first to address the matters I will be raising. As I was writing these letters, Ken Wareham called my attention to George Miller's delightful *Letters of a Hardboiled Teacher to His Half-baked Son*. This is a fine book, addressed to many of the same concerns as mine, and I recommend it to you, but unfortunately, published in 1931, it has long been out of print and some of his suggestions are dated as well. To provide some of its flavor, however, I have adopted some of Miller's revealing and trenchant comments to serve among other quotations as letter-headings. You met the first at the beginning of this Foreword.

In fact, this is not even the first book I have written on this subject. In 2015 I wrote *Letters to a Young Math Teacher*, which has already gone through two editions. Many teacher educators urged me to widen my sights because so much of that book applies to all teachers. Because I had also taught English and history courses, where indeed what I had written applied, I decided to prepare this book. But this is not simply an updated version of what I wrote in 2015. I have deeply revised some letters, in particular, the one on discipline, based on significant changes in the climate of our schools.

In this paragraph and in the letters that follow, there will be lots of I's. I have chosen to write these letters in the first person to convey the writer as a colleague. I offer no apology for this because these are highly personal communications. Remember, however, that many of them introduce my personal opinions. I encourage you not simply to accept my ideas, but instead to confront my opinions and those of others who have contributed their ideas to this book with your own. Even if, when doing so thoughtfully, you reject some of mine, both you and I will be well served. My goal in this book is to make your entrance into the real world of teaching better informed and therefore more comfortable; it is not to proselytize.

I have included in the Appendix a review of what I consider my qualifications to write these letters.

Acknowledgments

Appreciation is a wonderful thing.
It makes what is excellent in others
belong to us as well.
— Voltaire

Many people have played a role in the writing of this book. Some offered suggestions, others prepared content that I have attempted to cite appropriately in the letters, still others read and commented on drafts, often adding pertinent material, suggesting different approaches and correcting my errors.

Here is an alphabetical list of those who contributed to my thinking about this important subject. I apologize at the outset to the many I have still missed.

Samuel Alessi, Raul Amstelveen, Cynthia Anhalt, Agnes Azzolino, Dipendra Bhattacharya, Greg Baugher, Patti Brosnan, Steve Brown, Mary Bruton, the CCSSI staff, Doug Clements, Yong Colen, Art DiVito, Rodney Doran, Barry Garelick, Steve Greenberg, Danielle Goodwin, Barbro Grevholm, Geoffrey Gross, Jeffrey Hall, Marie Hone, Ken Jensen, Burt and Terry Kaufman, Jim and Susan Kelch, Genevieve Knight, Betty Krist, Linda Levi, Cheryl Lubinski, Craig McBride, David McMayer, Mike Morissette, Demetria Murray, William Parks, Ray Patenaude, Winnie Peterson, Peter Rowlett, Julie Sarama, Cathy Schloemer, Eileen Schoaff, James Schultz, Janet Shiver, Melanie Shores, Murray Siegel, Janet Stramel, Edward Strauser, Melanie Tait, Nermina Tanovic, John Titolo, Connie Toepfer, Dan Van der Vieren, John Ward and Ken Wareham.

I thank each of these people, but I also note that their inclusion on this list does not commit them to this final product. I accept responsibility for the outcome and only hope that I have lived up to at least some of their high expectations.

How to Read this Book

> *"Begin at the beginning,"* the King said, very gravely,
> *"and go on till you come to the end: then stop."*
> —Lewis Carroll

I follow an unusual format in writing this book. I focus the first letters on what I consider the most compelling features of the great adventure of taking responsibility for a school teaching assignment. In other words, I have adopted information priority for listing the letters. In this I follow the journalistic pattern of the newspaper article: get the key information out first, the details later.

But this is not the logical order. Reading first the lower priority personal letters, Ten through Twelve, provides a basis for those earlier ones.

Another way to think of this relates to the time available. If you begin reading this book a few months before teaching, follow the logical approach of the previous paragraph. Then read those first letters within weeks of entering the classroom.

And finally, read the other chapters at your leisure.

If, on the other hand, you have only a few days to delve into this book before taking on that assignment, do read those first chapters first, the others the first chance you get.

THE REAL WORLD

Letter One: My First Day

> *If ignorance of the real tricks
> of the teaching trade were a crime,
> you should be shot at sunrise.*
> —George Miller

    I had moved to Warsaw, New York to teach at the central high school there from my parents' home in Rochester just one day earlier. In this rural village about fifty miles southwest of Rochester and an equal distance southeast of Buffalo, I had found a room to rent in a lovely private home. As I was moving in I met my colleague, Roy Ketchum, who would be the school's new science teacher. His room was down the hall from mine and we shared a bathroom.

    When the first day of school arrived, I doubt that I had slept five minutes the previous night. Lying half awake I had confronted questions that seemed all to have the form, "What if the students...?" or "What if the principal...?" or "What if I...?", to none of which I had satisfactory answers.

    Roy and I had arranged an alternating plan for use of the bathroom that worked out fine on this beautiful fall morning. I was to go first that morning, which posed no problem as I was so nervous I could not have stayed in bed a moment beyond the sound of my alarm. We headed out together to walk through the small town to school. On the way, as planned, we stopped at Grover's Restaurant to have breakfast.

    We sat in a booth where a waitress served us. Then much to our surprise, the restaurant owner, Don Grover, came over to introduce himself. "I think you are two of our new teachers," he said. And so we discovered one of the characteristics of teaching in a small rural community: we were immediately members of that community. We would learn that this has both advantages — we would be *invited* to participate in town activities — and disadvantages — we would be *expected* to participate in town activities.

But neither of us thought about those things on this morning. As we finished our breakfast, I took my necktie from my pocket and put it on. I had waited to do this, knowing that otherwise, I would surely spill on it. So recently a college student, I was not comfortable even in this informal apparel.

On to the school a hundred yards down South Main Street.

Both of us had visited town earlier so we knew the general school layout and our contracts had told us the location of our classrooms and our subject assignments. This was a K-12 central school, drawing students from as far as twenty-five miles. As a newcomer, my schedule included a seventh-grade homeroom, two seventh grade classes, two ninth-grade classes and an honors course for seniors. In addition to that homeroom group, I was to spend one period each day monitoring a study hall.

I had been given copies of the three texts my students would be using and had studied them over the weeks since I was hired. My sense was that my greatest challenge would be the honors class, as the text included topics I had never met in college. As would soon become clear, this was my first of many misjudgments common to beginners.

Roy and I found our newly assigned mailboxes from which we picked up the school announcements. Several teachers introduced themselves and I immediately recognized what was to be one of my most serious teaching problems: I am very poor at remembering names. Faces are easy: I know who people are, but I have trouble assigning names to faces. This would haunt me for my entire teaching career. "If I have trouble remembering these few teachers' names, what will I do with those of over a hundred students?" I thought. And indeed that would be a problem for me until the end of my teaching days.

    I headed up to my classroom where I checked the cabinets for the books I would issue for the various courses. I worried that I wouldn't have enough.

    The buses arrived and students began to swarm into my homeroom. "Find a seat," I shouted over the clamor. Second mistake. It took me years to learn that your best bet is to keep your voice down even if it means dealing with each student individually. This did get the students' attention, however, and after a few minutes, they were all seated at desks. I went through the attendance register I had been provided. Of course, there were students whose names were not in the register and there were listed students missing. I would have to check on them later. Then I read to the students the announcements that had appeared in my mailbox.

    No sooner had I completed those tasks when a bell rang and the students raced off to their first period classes. Meanwhile, other students began to enter for my first class, in the process jamming the doorway against the last students making their way out. I noticed how the younger students gave way to their older classmates. As in most schools, there was an informal pecking order associated with the students' year in school.

    I was less than a half hour into the school day and I already felt myself sweating, my nerves on edge. How was I going to make it through another six hours of this?

    Classes were shortened to allow time for a school assembly at the end of this first day for the students in grades 7-12. This meant that I had only 25 minutes instead of the usual 45 minutes of class time. I took attendance and passed out the textbooks in each class. We had been told to wait until the next school day to start instruction, so I did nothing else and I even failed to assign seats in order to identify students. More among my litany of beginner's errors.

Next came my first seventh grade class with many students I had already met in my homeroom. These young boys and girls were even more noisy this period than they had been in that homeroom. I would soon learn that I had my initial assessment of teaching difficulty reversed. These seventh graders would be far tougher to work with than the seniors to whom I would be teaching far more difficult content. Even the ninth grade students, only two years older, would be more willing to get down to work.

I didn't think of it then but those youngsters were like all students: they were testing the limits of behavior they could get away with. I had certainly done that as a student myself and I had gone over the edge far too many times;[1] perhaps this behavior was serving as a kind of pay-back.

It was in this class that I had the first of my two odd experiences on this first day. One student was obviously older than his classmates. He seemed especially friendly and smiled constantly, but he acted strangely. He raised his hand often and when I finally called on him he announced, "Twenty-six," a number that had nothing to do with what was going on in the classroom. I soon realized that the boy was mentally challenged and I would somehow have to find a way to do my best for him. I simply replied, "Thank you," smiled at him and went on with what I was doing.

---

[1] My own worst year was sixth grade, the last year when we had the same teacher all day long. I was kept after school every single day that school year. If I had been treated then as too many students are today, I would have been identified as ADHD and would surely have been tranquilized. How that would have affected my academic achievement I have no idea.

If that episode had happened in my classroom when I was a seventh-grade student, we would all have roared with laughter. We were insensitive to the feelings of any individual student. Here, although there were a few giggles, most of the students were clearly accustomed to this boy's odd behavior Despite the difficulties I was having and would continue to have in working with these young boys and girls, I honor them for their behavior toward this challenged classmate.

When these students headed off to their next class, I slumped down at my desk. This was to be my planning period: a half hour to organize my thinking about the classes to come. But my mind drew a blank: I was unable to make any sense of what had already transpired. I had "gotten through" my first two classes and the students did not seem antagonistic to me, but in the second period especially they were noisy and seemed barely in control. I had again found myself having to talk over background chatter. I found myself nervous and irritated and this break in no way prepared me better for what was to come.

That break quickly over, the seniors filed in quietly and served a far better palliative than had that planning period. It was like meeting a group of human beings after trying to manage a zoo. I knew that the content I was teaching this class would be more challenging as some of it would be new to me, but I now felt more comfortable with that. I would remain for that full year a day or two ahead of my students, making content mistakes but able to work through those errors. I had completely misjudged which classes would be most difficult and I would look forward to this period each day.

This would also normally be my last morning class but the squeezed schedule meant that my afternoon ninth graders would meet now. This session went better and, reflecting on it, I realize now that I relaxed during that class of older students and that settled me down from the tension I had experienced earlier.

On to lunch. Mrs. Albro, an older woman who taught in the classroom next to mine, made a point of introducing herself and walking with me down to the student cafeteria. The cafeteria was noisy but in reasonable order. Experienced teachers had been assigned lunchroom duty that first week and they were getting students into acceptable routines, some of whom were passing down the line for school prepared lunches, others eating food brought from home. I would have my turn at monitoring these young diners in a few weeks.

Lunch turned out to be a pleasant interlude. Mrs. Albro showed me how we teachers were expected to break into the cafeteria line to be served — the students expected this politely — and we received generous portions from the pleasant servers. She then led me to the room set aside for teachers.

There I met more new colleagues. One immediately asked me how I liked working with seventh graders. I told him that I might be able to deal with them after about five years of experience. He laughed and warned me, "If you are going to tell a joke in a middle school class, be sure to tell it at the end of the period. Then they'll laugh all the way through the next teacher's class instead of yours." That insightful suggestion was a perfect lesson for my first day.

After the lunch break, my second seventh-grade math class filed in. This was another exuberant group and in this class I had my second odd experience. At its conclusion as their classmates were leaving, three boys came up to my desk. One of them spoke up shyly: "I'm epileptic and sometimes I have seizures. If one of them happens in class, don't worry. My friends here know what to do." I was so shocked by this that all I could say was, "Very good. I'm sorry about your problem and I'll remember that." But thank goodness, I thought, these twelve-year-olds can take such responsibility. Perhaps after all, they aren't the monsters I had already begun to consider them.[2]

Next, my study hall. Thankfully, I had been prepared for this assignment by the principal before the school year commenced.

Consider this. The study hall room, which also served as the school auditorium in this old school, was as big as a basketball court. In fact, the basketball court was directly above it on the school's third floor! The big room contained 240 double seats: eight rows of thirty seats in each row. My desk stood before them on a raised stage.[3]

This time my sergeant's voice did work for me. As the students forced their way in through the two doors, I announced several times, "Seniors on the window side, seventh graders near the door. The rest in between in class order." And as soon as I identified two seniors from my earlier class I had them help getting the students into reasonably ordered seats. Thankfully there were only about 150 students in this group so we could separate them into class sections with each student taking up one of those double seats.

Remarkably, within about five minutes the room was quiet enough that we could hear the rumbling of feet through the ceiling as students ran up and down the gymnasium above us. Before the bell rang I told the students that they must find and take the same seat the next day — when I would be making out a seating chart.[4]

---

[2] This unfortunate boy had no seizures in my classroom. He did in others, however, and I learned years later that he died in an accident. Trying to keep up with his friends, he fell from a high barn rafter.

[3] I would substitute (miserably) in the role of Scrooge on this stage at Christmastime when the student actor assigned the role had to be hospitalized. The entire student body was in attendance: two to a seat. The experience served me as an education in stage fright.

[4] Managing this study hall could be a serious problem. Later in the year I came upon an elderly Spanish teacher, whom I highly regarded, standing outside the room door sobbing. When I asked her what was wrong, she told me that she simply could not handle this assignment. "Give me a minute," I told her and

Once again I proved my predictions about teaching difficulties to be wrong. Managing this study hall was not the impossible task I had thought it would be.

My final class before the assembly was my second freshman class. Already excited about the coming assembly, this group was almost as bad as those seventh graders. I would soon realize how much harder it is to teach any subject late in the school day. If only all classes could be scheduled the first period in the morning, I suspect that the world would be twenty percent better educated.

In this class I did indeed run two books short and had to make do. Remarkably, the students were unfazed by this and pairs agreed to share. I learned later that this kind of thing happened often and the accepted rule was that, when the new book arrived, the students involved would flip a coin to see who would get it. So volunteering to share was not an entirely altruistic activity.

Now on to the assembly, this one held outside on the school grounds. Fortunately, I had no role to play and simply observed. I was relieved, however, at not being introduced to the student body.

Back to homeroom very briefly before dismissal for the day. And with the students gone, for the second time that day I collapsed into the chair behind my homeroom desk.

How in the world would I manage another 170 days of this? Never mind that: how would I just get through until the weekend?

Forcing myself up, I headed down to the athletic field where I would spend the next three hours in another of my roles: as an assistant football coach for the Warsaw Tigers.

---

walked into the noisy room. There I called up four seniors, two from my advanced algebra class, the other two football players. "I'll give you two minutes to get this room in order," I told them, "and from now on serve as a model for these kids instead of an instigator." In less than those two minutes we stood before a silent room and, needless to say, I had become a hero to one of my colleagues.

But as I walked out of my classroom I found myself taking a more positive philosophical approach to my situation. Yes, I had made some serious errors in my teaching, but I was making it through my first day and I had achieved something important to me.

I was now a high school teacher.

Letter Two: The Teaching Task

> *What office is there which involves more responsibility, which requires more qualifications, and which ought, therefore, to be more honorable than teaching?*
> —Harriet Martineau *Teaching in a Secondary School*

Consider the task you take on as a new teacher when you accept a secondary school teaching assignment. Here are the responsibilities of a typical newcomer in an American public school:

You will teach between 120 and 150 students in five classes. Those classes will not all be the same subject: you'll have two or three different so-called subject preps or preparations. In each of these classes you will be expected to organize the instructional program, present new content in class, develop and correct homework assignments, and evaluate your students. In doing so you will be expected, of course, to maintain acceptable discipline. You will be assigned a homeroom with another 25-30 students and a study hall to supervise with at least that many. If you are fortunate, you will teach all these classes in your homeroom, but some of you will be "roller skate" teachers, expected to teach each of your classes in a different classroom. You'll have a single period set aside for preparation. And you'll have a lunch break when you don't have a lunchroom supervision assignment.

Now think about that assignment. Who else among your fellow graduates takes on this level of responsibility? Most will head off to take jobs in which they are responsible only for themselves. New salesmen, office workers, scientists, lawyers, doctors or engineers, for example, do not supervise dozens of colleagues. A recently graduated military officer may command a platoon, but he or she will have experienced non-coms — army or marine sergeants and corporals or navy petty officers — to take major responsibility for their few dozen charges.

Is the assignment even doable? Consider homework and tests. Every minute you spend correcting each of your students' papers means an hour to an hour and a half of your time. Some teachers develop plans and tests they use year after year (an approach open to criticism); as a newcomer, you won't have that short-cut. And you will constantly have quite reasonable demands on your time by individual students. Unless you devote every minute of your waking day to your teaching program, you will end up forced to cut corners.

But what corners? Do you curtail preparation time and end up "winging it" in your classes? Do you reduce homework correction to the point that students know they do not need to spend time preparing it? Or do you end up with no life of your own?

That is the job you are undertaking. Recognize that the going will be rough, especially in your first year as you are accommodating to your school setting and your students are accommodating to you as well. Some of you won't make it. The claim that one of five will fail is overblown but that won't matter if you are one of those in trouble.

Yes, this is a tough job and you should not be hesitant to let those who are so critical of our schools know what you face.

But if you end up a successful classroom teacher, you will have much to be proud of.

Teaching in an Elementary School

Rather than detail the long list of responsibilities of an elementary school teacher, I offer two stories.

I was very fortunate to have Alice Foley as my teacher in fourth grade and then again in tenth grade to which she had transferred to teach high school English. She went on to become a school administrator and held some important state offices. When I returned to teach in the school from which I had graduated — Brighton High School in a Rochester, New York suburb — I met her once again. No longer my teacher, she was now one of my administrators. Despite all those interactions with her, I recall little about Miss Foley. I would not even be able to identify her in a photo and I recall nothing about her classroom instruction. But I do remember one episode. It took place at a party that celebrated one of her many achievements.

We were briefly paired off in conversation and I took advantage of that time together to ask her a question: "You know, Alice, you are the one teacher I know who has taught both elementary and secondary school classes. Which do you consider harder?" As a smug secondary school teacher then, I was confident what her answer would be, but I was fooled.

She quickly replied, "That's easy. There is no comparison. Elementary school teaching is much harder work."

Needless to say, I was taken aback by her response and at the time I wondered if she was just teasing me. I was even irritated by her answer. That was so long ago — before teacher unions entered the picture — when elementary school teachers were paid less than secondary school teachers. And I had found that quite acceptable. It was not until many years later when I supervised teachers at both levels and taught in some elementary school classrooms myself that I came to understand Miss Foley's evaluation.

Now skip ahead eight years. I am now the K-14 math coordinator for the Norwalk, Connecticut public schools and I am asked to organize a program for the school board about our mathematics teaching. I decide that the best way to do this will be to involve some of our classroom teachers. It is easy to pick senior high school and junior high school teachers, but I want to include elementary school teachers as well. The system-wide reading consultant suggests a third-grade teacher and a kindergarten teacher. I contact them and ask to visit their classes.

The third-grade teacher's lessons are well organized and quite creative. She clearly knows her students individually and draws from them the concepts she seeks to share. I am impressed. But I am still more impressed with the kindergarten teacher. When I talked to her before visiting, she warned me that she was not one of those who saw kindergarten as what she called "the first step in the road to the SATs." When I ask her to explain what she means, she tells me that she feels that it is more important to provide children at this age with experiences that relate to their own lives rather than push first grade down one year.

And when I visit her classroom, she shows me what she meant by that. I am there to see math-related activities so she manages her two dozen children like a ringmaster, involving them in what I consider perfect math for that age. She has the students pair off to march around the room then regroup by threes, she has them assign one, two and three to the individual members of each group and she then has the groups change, the ones, twos and threes going to different parts of the room. She has them match the snack items to the number of students in the room – no counting involved;

instead, she asks questions like Do we have enough? Too few? Too many? And these kinds of activities continue for over an hour. Terms like add and subtract are never mentioned but activities related to addition and subtraction with physical objects build readiness for those ideas to be formalized later.

All I could think of when I finally left that classroom was that our schools would be better served if this kind of activity could be continued up through at least the primary grades. (I was reminded of the experiment carried out in some New Hampshire elementary schools in the early 1900s. No teaching of specific arithmetic concepts and skills was allowed until sixth grade but a year later the students were doing just as well as those in the standard program. For a description of this experiment, see Benezet's account listed in the bibliography.)

And that was just math. When I returned to my district office and told the language arts coordinator about my experience, he told me that she had similarly impressed him with activities in support of his goals.

I came away from each of those classes exhausted from simply watching the performances of teachers and students. What I had seen in each was carefully planned activity. And in both those activities changed every few minutes so there were many of them with an equal number of transitions, those points in any lesson where it is so easy to lose the attention or even control of a class.

Those experiences provided chapter and verse for Alice Foley's response. Of course, many elementary school teachers would have difficulty teaching advanced high school topics and the homework and test correcting loads are certainly different, but I would be hard pressed to last ten minutes on my own in one of their classrooms.

You and the Public Perception of Your Profession

Recent polls show respect for teachers in the United States

is not only low compared with many other countries but even declining. That is indeed unfortunate, but it is beside the point as far as you are concerned. The important message I have tried to convey in this letter is that you should recognize the challenge of the career on which you are setting out and appreciate what accomplishing it means. Do not think of yourself as a small cog in the educational establishment:

rather, understand that, if you master the task you undertake, you will be meeting the requirements of a very tough job.

Letter Three: The School Environment

> *What you learned will not hurt you;*
> *but I want to invite your attention*
> *to what you did not learn.*
> —George Miller

You are on your own!

This is the first thing you must recognize about school teaching. No matter what your training or background, when the students troop into your classroom and you close the door, you and they are shut off from the rest of the world.

The Downside

One way of thinking about this is as a confrontation with your students. It is you against them and they have the numbers on their side. It's twenty or thirty to one here and you must use every trick of the trade to fend off the lions.[5,6]

Another way to consider your situation is in terms of your responsibility. Somehow you have to change each of these youngsters. You have to remake them into independent thinkers about the material you and they will address.

Thought of in these terms, your assignments (four to six of these classes) may seem overwhelming.

---

[5] It is sad to note that, if they set out to do so, students can not only make life miserable for teachers but they can even force teachers out of education. For example, they can spread stories about physical contact. Thankfully such episodes are rare but they do happen. See, for example, Letter Seven.

[6] Even worse, as I write this, newspaper headlines announce the death of a popular Massachusetts teacher shot by a student.

Will you have help in addressing your responsibilities? Don't count on it. In fact, in most schools not only will you receive no help whatsoever but it will soon seem that the administration is working against you. Your class will be interrupted by announcements, individual students will be called out of class, fire drills will seem timed to occur during class tests and classes will be unexpectedly canceled for school activities like pep rallies. Simple instruction will seem always to take a back seat.

But wait a minute. Didn't the school principal tell you before classes began that he and his assistants were available if you need them?

You must recognize that there are problems with this offer of help. Consider a standard scenario: you have a series of problems with Horace. Day after day you put up with this student's shenanigans. Finally, at wit's end you send this youngster to the school discipline officer. The student returns with a note he hands you, a grin on his face. It says: "I have told Horace to behave."

More important, you have sent to your administration a negative message about yourself. Why weren't you able to handle this student? Too many of these referrals, no matter how bad the offense, how wicked the offender, and your status and even your job may be threatened.

Sadly, in most schools the attitude of the school administration seems to be that discipline counts above all else, with learning far back in the crowd. If you can keep the lid on your classes, no matter how you do so, you will be recognized as a good teacher.

In fact, if you handle your own discipline, you will rarely receive supervisory or evaluative visits from administrators. Perhaps my own experience was exceptional, but my classrooms were visited less than a half dozen times in all my years of school classroom instruction.[7]

Until, that is, exam results are posted. Only then will any lack of achievement count against you.

Yes, all that is true but there are other ways of considering your work.

The Upside

You have been given a quite remarkable opportunity. You may be a half dozen or even fewer years older than the students assigned to you, but you can work with these students in the ways *you choose*. Despite your age and lack of experience, you're the boss. When you close that classroom door you are in charge. Instead of being told what to do — almost your entire experience up until now — the tables are turned and you do the telling.

Yes, you have serious responsibilities but they represent challenges. You can test yourself against those challenges and grow in the process.

And I promise you that no matter what grade you teach, you will learn. You will find yourself saying over and over, "If only I had known that when I was a student," and "Why didn't I understand that when I was studying it?"

Consider the legal terminology: *in loco parentis*. This phrase — in place of a parent — represents another way of considering your role. You're serving in the classroom as a temporary substitute mother or father of these youngsters. The phrase is often used — by the courts, for example — to blame people in settings like yours for abusing the role, but you should consider it an honor to be assigned such an opportunity by our society.

You should recognize too how important you are to these

---

[7] There is a real sense in which I was shortchanged by this lack of supervisory visits. I am sure now in retrospect that I could have gained from such oversight. Interestingly, when one of my students read this paragraph, his response was, "I finally realize the source of your shortcomings."

adolescents. During the school year, they will see almost as much of you and your teaching colleagues as they will of their parents. Your conduct will strongly influence their view not only of the subject you teach but of the society in which they live as well.

And at least you will have 150 or more days to accomplish something. Any undertaking divided by 150 becomes far more reasonable. Of course you will make mistakes, of course things will go wrong, but you will have plenty of opportunities to make up for those errors.

Letter Four: Before You Start

> *Spectacular achievement is always preceded by unspectacular preparation.*
> —Robert H. Schuler

When I asked experienced teachers why they think that teachers fail, I received the following interesting response from Roger Fisher:

I worry about teachers going into classrooms without a comprehensive plan for classroom management. By "classroom management," I don't mean a euphemism for "classroom discipline," although that's important too. I worry more about the minutiae of daily classroom procedures. What do students do when they come in? Where do they put completed assignments? What is the policy for late assignments? When do progress reports go out? How will I keep track of those students whose grades are poor, and how will I communicate this information to parents before progress reports go out? How do I check out textbooks? What happens if a student loses one? When I was a new teacher, I had no overarching plan for dealing with these issues, and to this day I still don't understand why I was so oblivious to something so obvious.

As my first day narrative should have made clear, I fit Roger Fisher's characterization of incompetent preparation perfectly. I had been recruited by the school principal, Gilbert Ball, in a telephone conversation. What I remember about that conversation was my surprise that I should be invited to teach math. I told Mr. Ball that I was an English major and had planned to teach that subject. "Never mind that," he responded, "You have taken enough courses to satisfy math certification requirements," as indeed I had because my undergraduate education during World War II was in an officer preparation program that required those courses. The face-to-face job interview that followed was a supper at the Ball home at which there was not one minute of job-related conversation. (I was, however, suitably impressed by the excellent meal and Ball's attractive daughters.) My contract offer came in the mail and after signing it I returned it the same way. It was from that contract that I learned the superficial details of my teaching assignment and the texts I would be using in my three preps.

So I showed up on that first day of school with answers to not one of Roger Fisher's questions. That I got away with starting without any attempt to answer those questions surprises me now just as the more general concern surprises him.

What harm did that lack of preparation do to my early weeks of teaching? In retrospect, I can see that my lack of prior preparation punished both me and my students. During those early weeks I certainly short-changed them as I wrestled on their dime with organizing my teaching.

Winging it is not the best way to do anything. Even those stand-up comedians who seem to be improvising as they interact with their audience have usually spent months developing their routines. Of course, they are adept at meeting unusual reactions from their audiences — you too should become equally adept over time — but they and you need a firm basis from which to work.

Yes, some teachers may be forced by circumstances to begin any teaching assignment with no prior knowledge of the setting into which they would be thrust. I didn't have that excuse and hopefully you will not have that excuse either.

What then should you do after you accept a teaching assignment? Surely there are some basics that you should seek to accomplish. Here are a few of the organizational questions you should think about seriously:

1. What are the specifics of the assignment: courses, textbooks, classroom location, arrangements for making copies of handouts and tests, the availability of technical equipment, even the check-in procedures in the school office and the location of your office mailbox?
2. How will you manage the distribution of textbooks?
3. How are students graded in this school?
4. Are students in multiple-section courses grouped by ability?

It should be clear that you will need help in answering many of those questions. You'll have to find a good source of answers. That source in larger schools might be your department head, in smaller schools the principal or vice principal. In many schools a senior member of the school secretarial staff can answer some of those questions for you. You will do yourself a service if you organize your questions carefully before approaching those busy people.

Beyond Specifics

But those are only some of Roger Fisher's questions. Others you must think about yourself. How are you going to structure your classes? How will you handle homework assignments and the work students prepare in response? In classrooms with moveable furniture, how are you going to arrange the seating? How are you going to learn your students' names? How do you plan to differentiate instruction for brighter and weaker students?

Some of you will have considered questions like these in

your teacher preparation programs, but now you need to come up with some thinking about the specific setting into which you are stepping. Now you're not answering those questions as part of a homework assignment; rather, you're answering them as they will affect your career.

Of course, Robert Browning had it right when he wrote, "The best-laid plans o' mice an' men Gang aft agley,"[8] and you will almost certainly have to modify your plans once they are confronted with your students. But modifying plans is much easier to accomplish when you have carefully designed plans to modify.

---

[8] This latter phrase is commonly translated as "go often wrong."

Letter Five: Discipline

> *We need to understand that*
> *discipline is something you do **for** a child.*
> *Punishment is something you do*
> ***to** a child when discipline fails.*
> —Zig Ziglar

This is, of course, the letter you have been waiting for: if I can show you how to gain and maintain classroom discipline, I will have solved THE major problem that besets all teachers.

Sorry Charleen and Charley but this is a problem for which there is no magic bullet. You must address this problem each year in each of your classrooms. Why? Because discipline is achieved by mastering many variables, most notably your personality and the personality of each of your individual students. There are many other things that influence discipline — your students' background, the culture of the community in which you teach, the content you are teaching, and so on — but the personalities in your classroom are far and away the most important.

No, I cannot give you answers and, in fact, my own classroom discipline was never to my satisfaction. Like most teachers I had successes and failures. I only offer suggestions that I believe can make a difference in your teaching.

I begin with what I consider the most important. You are probably now, as I was when I began teaching, only a very few years older than your students. You could very likely pass for one of them.[9] Even if you wish you were one of them, however, your role now is very different: you must act as an adult among adolescents. Even if you aren't sure that this new role fits you, you should adopt this posture.

Think of your situation this way. In any given classroom you will be one of, say, 26 young people. If you are simply one of that crowd, you're not going to do much teaching. You need to establish yourself as the leader of that group and you are going to have to accomplish that on your own. You have a lot going for you — in fact your students enter your classroom expecting you to be led by you — but you need to get out front to make use of your skills. The fact that you are the assigned teacher in this classroom gives you a head start, but you have to take advantage of the opportunity this offers or your students will soon catch up and may even pass you.

Establishing Distance

How can you distinguish yourself? First of all, dress with care: conservatively and neatly. When I taught, men were expected to wear neckties and sports jackets or suits, women to wear dresses. Today there appear to be no deportment rules and in particular, except in private and parochial schools where students wear neckties too, such expectations appear to be passé. Whatever the standards for teacher dress at your school, see to it that your clothing is neat and clean.

You may well have come from an environment where you dressed down to be accepted: with patched, torn and

---

[9] Having been a school student recently gives you some insight into the way students think and react. You don't need to refer to books like *High School Confidential* to see the worst of student behavior. In fact, you will do well to stay away from such books at least until you have settled into your role.

tie-dyed clothing the norm. And you will almost certainly meet students who fit that mold. But your goal now is not to be one of them. What you wear will send an important message.[10]

What you wear should identify you as an adult but, even more important, you must then live up to that identification. You should establish and maintain a distance from your students. A get-down-to-business and get-on-with-it approach will serve you well here.

Consider in this regard an experience I had early in my teaching career. As part of my teaching assignment in Johnson City, New York I was to serve as freshman football coach. On an early September afternoon I met with the head coach, Ed Butkis — a famous player himself, he had been one of a famous "seven blocks of granite" Fordham University line. Ed's school varsity at the time had won every game for five seasons.

Ed assigned me, the newest of his assistants, the task of closing up the locker room at the end of practice the first week. I brought my young players in for their showers late that afternoon only to come upon two giant first-string linemen, each half-again my size, wrestling between the lockers. Just as I entered, one of these monsters picked up his 250-pound teammate and threw him across the room. All I could think at the time was, "Perhaps I am in the wrong occupation." I pictured them turning their testosterone-driven energies on me. But I took what I thought might be my last breath and simply asked them to get dressed and get going. Much to my surprise they did exactly that and I breathed once again.

This illustrates what you have going for you. You are just

---

[10] I must note here that I would have rejected as silly this suggestion about the importance of clothing when I was a beginner. Only later was I happy that the then required dress codes had forced me to conform.

as new to your students as they are to you. Get out ahead of them and immediately set tasks for your students. That is the best message I can give you.

Here is a specific example of what I mean. Several of the schools I taught in began the school year with all-school assemblies that were an odd mix of rule-establishing followed by a spirit-raising pep-rally for the fall athletic teams. After this the students followed a much-abbreviated class schedule. We met our assigned groups for only about twenty minutes. The principals told us only to take attendance in order to set the year's schedule. Warsaw was only the first of these schools. To me this always seemed to be the worst way to start school: on the one day when most students were motivated to study, that drive was entirely compromised.

I followed those instructions only that first year. As I described in my first letter, I did try to spend the entire twenty minutes of each of those classes taking attendance, but by the end of those short periods the students were ready to jump out of the window. Not only was a school day wasted but I had lost an opportunity to establish myself with my classes. I had to regain authority in subsequent sessions.

After that one debacle, I never again followed those instructions. In each of my first classes I skipped taking attendance entirely. Later I would have an assigned student do that. Then that first day I quickly taught a carefully prepared lesson and gave an assignment. The difference was extraordinary. I gained far more than that one class head start: I gained stature with my students that served me well through the remainder of the year. I urge you to take that lesson to heart.

There is a well-known adage that experienced teachers often share with beginners: "Don't smile until Christmas." That may be a bit strong but you have not been hired to be eithr a stand-up comedian or the students' friend. Take your job very seriously is a better way of expressing that familiar adage. Doing so will help with discipline as well. Joking with your students can have a positive effect on your teaching once you have established yourself, but the time for that is definitely not early in your first year.

Most of what I have said until now relates to aspects of disciplining yourself in order to have a basis from which to discipline your students. Now what about those youngsters?

Disciplining Students

A bored student is very often a problem student. Ken Wareham addresses this as it relates to bright kids:

The worst thing a teacher can have is a smart student who is bored. Smart + bored = trouble, and left unchecked is a recipe for disaster. Oftentimes it is simply curiosity and deals with little things like talking when they have finished an assignment and disrupting those who are not done, or playing little practical jokes and pranks. I have memories that haunt me, where I wonder what I didn't do that could have kept a kid out of trouble — trouble which in some cases even finally devolved into alcohol or drugs, sex, or wrapping a car around a telephone pole.

I believe that Ken's concerns about bright students extends to all students. His message tells you to keep your classes moving and your students active.

Many people feel that men have through physical size and power an advantage over women in enforcing classroom discipline. Contradicting this, my general observation is that women do at least as well as men in managing their classes. This suggests to me that women are in many ways better at handling discipline than men. For that reason I take very seriously recommendations teacher Demetria Murray of Tucson, Arizona has communicated to me. Here is what she writes:

> My first recommendation is to discipline students with dignity. By this I mean:

1. Use proximity to help refocus students. If a student is off-task, casually move to that part of the room and position yourself near that student. Often, just being near the student is enough to stop the behavior without having to discuss it.

2. Incorporate off-task students into problems. For example, if Steve is paying more attention to Sarah in class instead of your lesson, you can say "The other day, Steve was telling me how much he likes to go to Home Depot. We're going to calculate how much paint Steve should buy if we want to repaint this classroom." This can bring the student's focus back onto the problem without having to stop your lesson.

3. Use private reminders and conversations to address behavior. Rather than standing at the front of the room and saying, "Amy, please stop talking to Caity," it is often more effective to lean down and ask Amy in a whisper to stop talking. Likewise, if you need to have more of an extended conversation with a student about his or her behavior, ask the student to step to a corner of the room, away from others. This privacy prevents the student from being embarrassed in front of the class, and often results in student cooperation.

My second recommendation comes from advice I received during my second year teaching from my assistant principal. She said, "Kids have power." She went on to say that you need to acknowledge their power and not engage in a battle with them. Rather, allow them to make a choice, but with that choice comes a consequence. For example, if Jen keeps putting her head down and not taking notes, you could first try using proximity and a private reminder. If those approaches fail, you could tell her the next time she chooses not to take notes, she will need to come in at lunch and copy them. Rather than getting into a power struggle, remain calm and communicate your expectations. Give students a choice about how they can change their behavior and in this way allow them to retain their power. Following this action plan will allow you to remain calm in potentially stressful situations.

Avoid the Need for Confrontations

I urge you to note the commonality of all of Ms. Murray's recommendations. They are designed to defuse rather than exacerbate situations. She also offers proactive suggestions:

1. Be (over)prepared. I know you've heard it before – "It's better to over-prepare than underprepare." But it is completely true when teaching. If you are organized with your lesson plan, provide clear directions, and keep students actively engaged and on-task, then your management issues will be greatly minimized.

2. Walk the trenches. Be out among your students. Don't stand at the board the whole time. Get out and see what your students are writing on their papers. Are they taking notes or writing love notes? Are they drawing geometric figures or what the back of your head looks like? Which students got the practice problems right that you assigned? What mistakes were they making?
    Where did they get stuck?
    You should be able to answer these questions and in doing so, you send a message to your students that they are going to be held accountable for the assignments you give them. This produces on-task behavior, which produces student success, which produces a happy teacher.

3. Be consistent. This applies to your rules and procedures

as well as between students. If you say it needs to be silent when class starts, then you need to enforce it. Letting a little conversation take place here and there sends a mixed message to students and before you know it, the whole room is talking and likely not about the math. Following through on what you say keeps your expectations clear.

I wish Ms. Murray had been a mentor to me when I was a beginner as she has been in her Flowing Wells School District in Tucson.

But beware. Ms. Murray is not providing scripts to memorize. She is offering general techniques that must be modified to fit the particular situations that arise in your classrooms. In fact, even if you find a particular technique that works for you, you will find that it will lose its power over time.

For example, if you suddenly interrupt class by saying to a student in the back of your room who is misbehaving, "Bill, come up here," it might well have a striking effect with all attention focused on Bill and you in a suddenly silent classroom. Why? Because what you did was unexpected. You could then simply whisper to Bill, "Thanks. Now take your seat again," and continue your teaching with a subdued group of students. However, if you do this again in the same class the next day, you will almost certainly have no such response. Your students were reacting to the uniqueness of the situation. In your teaching you will meet thousands of these episodes, so you need to place the specific Murray examples in the context of her more general management recommendations.

I cannot resist offering here an extreme example of an unexpected disciplinary action that did happen. A friend of mine was one of two physics teachers in a large school. In his class he had a student who irritated him with his bad conduct. Finally, he angrily said to the student, "Bill, I've had enough of your behavior in this class and I will have no more of it. Come with me," and he marched Bill down the hall to the classroom of the other physics teacher. Interrupting this instructor's class, he said to him, "I have here Bill, the worst student I have ever tried to teach. If you have one who is equally bad, please trade with me." His colleague responded, "I do indeed. Joe, I can't stand you any longer and want nothing more to do with you. Go with this teacher and keep out of my sight." And off my friend went with his new student.

Of course, what these teenagers and their classmates did not know was that this trade had been worked out beforehand between the teachers and with the blessing of the school guidance department. My friend told me that the exchange worked so well that both students improved in both deportment and achievement and that the episode had a general calming effect on both classes.

Raoul Amstelveen offers some interesting comments related to this. Here are some of the points he makes together with some additions of my own:

1. Teaching methods courses often offer material appropriate to honors classes. More often than not, as a beginner you will be assigned weaker students. Think seriously about these less able and less motivated students and prepare yourself to work with them.

2. Know your school's policies and develop your own with regard to discipline. Then adhere to them. Students appreciate consistency. And follow up on any serious disciplinary measures you take with the student and his or her counselors and parents.

3. Build your reputation with care. It is far easier over time to relax strict discipline than it is to strengthen weak discipline.

4. Be ready for the unexpected. Ask yourself what you can do about such things as: When a student criticizes you. When a student curses in class, especially when the student is using language that is standard in his society. When a parent complains about your behavior. When your class is interrupted.

Three More Points about Discipline

I recall reading the account of an urban classroom teacher[11] whose own class he could not control. His principal, in an attempt to help him find a way to regain control, had the teacher visit a neighbor's classes to see how good discipline was managed. He did so and indeed found a quiet, apparently well-disciplined group of students.

But what was going on in that class? When the students arrived, the teacher assigned them a task: write in detail about all the things you did since yesterday. The students wrote for the full class period, the only breaks coming when individuals asked permission to sharpen a pencil or go to the restroom. At the end of the class the teacher collected the papers and, as soon as the children had filed out the door, she dumped them in her wastebasket. The visiting teacher surreptitiously retrieved the papers from the trash and reviewed them. They were mostly illegible and strewn with pornographic cartoons and vulgar symbols. Clearly there was an understanding in that class between teacher and students: you don't bother me and I won't bother you.

Yes, you can attain "discipline" by techniques like that: you can give class quizzes that you discard just as did that English teacher, you can simply assign the next day's

---

[11] See Jonathan Kozol's *Death at an Early Age*.

homework, you can show movies, or you can even "give your students a day off." And, if you can keep the lid on such classes, your supervisors may even be satisfied – at least until test results are in. But you will be demeaning yourself if you do.

Second, I urge you to avoid like poison ivy any negative reference to gender or race and do not allow those topics to come up in your classrooms – or outside your classrooms as well. These topics not only represent sources of student embarrassment but any discussion of them is far too easily misconstrued to their – and your – disadvantage.[12] This topic is so important that I will address it in the next letter.

And don't stereotype your students in any way, even in joking — something silly like "you're a bunch of bad apples" — as students easily misconstrue and exaggerate such remarks. Subtlety is beyond many youngsters and that jesting remark could easily be translated to be "he doesn't like us" or even "he hates us."

The situation can be even worse. Raul Amstelveen has it right when he says, "Regardless how tempting it is, a teacher should *never demean, embarrass or humiliate* a student in front of his or her peers. This can leave life-long scars for those involved."

It may seem extreme but I suggest avoid touching students, even to give one of them a pat on the back for an accomplishment. This may seem extreme but, especially for new teachers, such contact can be exaggerated or wrongly identified by the student.

In one school district in which I served we teachers received a "greeting" communication from the district principal each year. This message also included a series of school rules, one of which was that we were never to have

---

[12] For some of the worst kind of cruel remarks see those by 18th century English dictionary writer and critic, Samuel Johnson. Many are recorded in James Boswell's famous biography.

physical contact with students. An example was included, "If a student tries to leave your classroom without your permission, can you block his or her exit? No." I recall that this incensed us teachers, but on reflection I think that the message was reasonable. Such a confrontation could easily get out of hand.

And third, if you get involved in school activities in out-ofclass activities as coach or club advisor, it will often help with classroom discipline. Students in those informal settings can get to know and appreciate you in different ways and their support can be useful.

Everyone knows the old adage: Count to ten before you make an important decision. Unfortunately, that does not apply here. While you're counting, the situation you need to address may spin out of control. Instead, you need not only to come up with responses, but you need to come up with them quickly. No wonder you will make mistakes. Hopefully you will learn from those mistakes and not simply repeat them. I close this letter with a perfect summary by Mike Morissette:

Be friendly, but not their friend. Kids already have enough friends and don't need another one. Trying to be their friend is asking for trouble. Your classroom management will suffer as a result and if you get too friendly, you may be accused of sexual assault. Along those lines, do not ever touch a student or be alone in your classroom with a student with your classroom door shut. As for the being friendly part, you'd be amazed at how much harder kids will try in your class if they know you genuinely care about them and their well-being. Go to their sporting events and plays. It means a lot to students to see their teachers in the stands.

Letter Six: Discrimination

> *While Title IX is best known for its impact on high school and collegiate athletics, the original statute made no explicit mention of sports.*
> — Wikipedia

The Patsy T. Mink Equal Opportunity in Education Act was signed into law as an amendment to the Civil Rights Act of 1964. It provided protection against discrimination based on race, color or national origin but excluded sex discrimination. That law was amended in 1972, however, to address this exception. Better known as Title IX, the amendment states simply: "No person in the United States shall, on the basis of sex, be excluded from participation in, be denied the benefits of, or be subjected to discrimination under any education program or activity receiving Federal financial assistance."

This law has had what I believe to be a very positive impact on our schools. Women's school and college sporting activities today would not be recognized by anyone living in 1970. If they even existed in schools before the act, they received no fiscal support.

As I noted in Letter Six, you should be sensitive to every one of those areas — race, color, national origin and gender — in your classroom instruction. While giant strides have been made in each of those areas,[13] we still have some distance to

---

[13] As just two personal examples, when I served in the navy during World War II, the only role open to blacks on my ship was as servants to us officers and, of course, we had not a single woman aboard. If through some kind of time warp one of my shipmates then could visit any ship today, he would be dumbfounded.

go.

I address in this letter an example of sex discrimination, but the ideas apply to each of those other areas.

Consider the following story. It is essentially true but I have modified it in order to protect the individual involved.

A friend of mine was one of the finest classroom instructors I know. That is not only my view as an outsider but that of many of his students over the years. He won teaching awards from his students as well as his colleagues. But after over twenty years of what had been considered effective classroom teaching and coaching, he was forced to accept early retirement as an offender of Title IX. Instead of leaving his profession with honors, he retired dishonored.

This man was not a sex offender in the sense we usually consider it. He never had an affair with a student or any hint of such conduct. But as a result of his leaving his position in the way he did, many people condemn him as a sexual predator.

How did this happen?

On a field trip to Washington, D.C., one of his students came to him with a companion to complain of being very uncomfortable physically. He explained to the student some possible responses to her condition, which the student and her friend unfortunately considered in bad taste. They reported his behavior to the school guidance counselor who, with the school principal convened a committee to investigate the matter. Meanwhile the teacher was required to take a paid leave of absence and excluded from the school campus.

The counselor interviewed not only the two girls but also other students who had gone on this and other earlier field trips that this teacher had chaperoned. Pressed for examples of marginal behavior, several other young women gave examples that had made them uncomfortable. One example: the teacher had straightened a young woman's collar when the group was going out to dinner. Another commented that the teacher had commended her on her poise.

All these interviews were done supposedly in secret, but of course other students soon learned the gossip that their teacher was in trouble. But they did not know what was the offense: had the teacher seriously compromised a student? Despite that possibility, a number of students approached the school administration in support of the teacher.

Realizing how serious the matter had become, the teacher hired a lawyer who specialized in Title IX defense at a cost of over $10,000. This attorney negotiated an agreement with the school to have no charges brought; however, the teacher would not be allowed to return to the school. He would have to retire "in good standing" at the end of that school year, but was paid for an additional year. Finally he had to agree not to disclose anything about his case.

Although it is reasonable to read that story as a defense of my friend and my description certainly favors him, I do not offer it as a defense. Quite the contrary, I do so as a warning about how guarded must be your behavior when dealing with students whose sex — and equally their race, color or national origin — differs from your own, and in some cases even if it is the same as yours.

This episode was unpleasant not only for this teacher but for the school authorities who felt compelled to act and certainly for the students involved as well. If you disagree with how this was handled, you should ask yourself how you would have done so. Furthermore, Title IX has developed a federal bureaucracy that oversees such cases and failure on the part of the school to act as they did would have led to further trauma.

I am old enough to have taught in a school which had two entrances: one labeled "Boys" the other "Girls". I strongly support Title IX and the other civil rights legislation. They were long overdue. But we continue to live in a time of transition that will extend well into the future. And during that time our behavior must not only meet normal social standards but must be even further constrained.

Some take-aways from this episode:
- Recognize that in all settings, in school and outside the school building as well, your behavior toward the students of your school must be as their teacher.
- While it is important that you work one-to-one with individual students, be sensitive to settings when you are alone with them. At the very least leave your classroom door open when doing so. If you tutor a student outside of school do so in a public setting like a public library.
- Avoid touching students.
- Do not call attention to your students' dress or appearance. This includes praise as well as criticism.
- Be especially careful with humor. Much humor has a bullying quality and that should be strictly avoided.
- Recognize that unless you are a saint, you are prejudiced and you must deal with your prejudices. That is a far better approach than pretending somehow to be fair and equal to everyone without exception.

Now having provided you with a worst-case scenario, I want to place this in perspective. Yes, there are some constraints to your behavior to which you should be aware and student characteristics to which you should be especially sensitive, but those constraints are really very minor.

And you almost certainly make mistakes. If you do, I urge you to apologize immediately not only to any student involved but also to the class in general.

Letter Seven: Textbooks and Curriculum Revision

> *Within a couple of years, we start testing*
> *on standards we're not teaching*
> *with curriculum we don't have*
> *on computers that don't exist.*
> —Randi Weingarten

As noted earlier, your classroom assignment will usually include several different subjects to teach. Your students and you will usually be provided textbooks for each of those courses, your copy probably including exercise answers. You may also be given locally prepared curriculum guides or courses of study for those teaching responsibilities.

Your central task is to teach that content to your students. That is a serious and difficult undertaking and you should keep focused on it. That may seem obvious to you, but some people think that the tasks of teachers relate more to the development of social skills.

The most important tool for your teaching, I believe, is your textbook. Of course textbooks vary in quality and are open to criticism, but you will find that they will provide a basis upon which you can organize your instructional program.

I once initiated a semester course for high school seniors and prepared a local text for it. Each night I wrote the halfdozen or so pages and I then photocopied them for the students to use.[14] I strongly discourage you from undertaking such a project. While I enjoyed the experience and the student response was very positive, it was extremely time and energy consuming and, most important, it took away from those same qualities that I was able to devote to my regular teaching assignments. I found myself forced to cut far too many corners in my classroom instruction.

My point here is simply that you should keep your focus on your central task. If you choose to do other things, they should cut into whatever spare time you have and not into the time you devote to your teaching. My experience writing that textbook added to the breadth of my knowledge, but even that was non-instructional activity.

Instead I urge you to rely on the text assigned to your course as a basic organizing tool. Especially as a beginning teacher, you will be well served in that reliance. This does not mean, however, that you should be tied to the details found in that text. I will have more to say on that score in my letter about organizing your daily instruction.

In fact, I found it very useful in planning my lessons to refer also to a second text that covers the same material. A colleague once placed this suggestion in a different light: "Don't assign the best text for your students," he told me. "Instead give them a pedestrian text and use the best one you can find to prepare your teaching." While that self-serving recommendation may be unfair to authors, it represents an interesting point of view that you might want to consider if you ever find yourself responsible for choosing a text. Whether you act on it or not, using a second text as a reference can serve you well in providing different approaches to concepts, different examples, different exercises and added background.

In three of the schools in which I taught, we teachers were organized by the school administers into teams to write

---

[14] I was somewhat disconcerted when I returned to visit that school thirty years later to learn that the textual materials I had prepared were still being used.

curricula for our various courses. This, it seemed to me at the time — and still seems to me today — to have been a complete misuse of our time. Recognizing the uselessness of the task, we simply copied the chapters of the texts we were using to serve as course outlines. Our products were bound and from that time on our own copies resided in desk drawers gathering dust. Of course, our administrators proudly distributed these nonsensical "Courses of Study" to school board members as another of their achievements.

When I became a school department head and later a city math coordinator, I made those required but value-free tasks my responsibility and insisted that classroom teachers spend their meetings on instructional improvement: sharing such things as teaching materials and techniques as well as background information about students.[15]

Changing Curricula

Today much is made of the controversial Common Core curriculum standards English/language arts and mathematics. Similar curriculum change is going on in other disciplines as well. This redirection of school instruction is having a profound effect on classroom teaching but, once again, it should not be the role of the classroom teacher to translate those standards into instructional materials. To respond to these standards, teachers should be provided textual materials on which to base their teaching.

It is not my intent here to argue for or against those standards. I believe that they have both positive and negative features. I will, however, address one concern in this letter about assessment. What bothers me about the approach of curriculum innovators are statements like the following:

---

[15] Warning: It is easy for me to criticize these activities so much loved by administrators. I would not do so as a beginning teacher.

The Common Core State Standards provide a consistent, clear understanding of what students are expected to learn, so teachers and parents know what they need to do to help them.

Hardly. I offer a specific example. Choosing from among the hundreds of specific standards I offer one of the most straightforward: Among the mathematics standards under the heading "Solve systems of equations" appears this student expectation:

> 6. Solve a simple system consisting of a linear equation and a quadratic equation in two variables algebraically and graphically. *For example, find the points of intersection between the line $y = -3x$ and the circle $x^2 + y^2 = 3$.*[16]

It is not important (unless you are a math teacher) that you understand what that particular standard is talking about to follow what I have to say about it.

Any math teacher could make up a lesson or lessons related to accomplishing that standard. But in doing so that teacher would need to prepare not only what would be presented in class but also the exercises to be assigned for homework and any written material that students could use outside class to review the topic. While those are reasonably straightforward tasks, they take a considerable amount of time from an already crowded day and they are exactly the kinds of tasks that are normally supplied to teachers by textbooks.

Fortunately, today textbooks that reflect these new expectations are being produced but further delays in providing them for many classroom teachers are due to the strain that new text adoption places on school budgets. Given the pace of school curriculum reform that

---

[16] *Common Core State Standards for Mathematics*, page 65-66, www.corestandards.org/assets/CCSSI_Math%20Standards.pdf

I have witnessed over the years, I expect that by the time the new curricula have been fully implemented, another round of change will be demanded of teachers. And once again they will be expected to address them without appropriate support.

In fact, are the new texts even appropriate to the new curricula? Be prepared for a deluge of false claims by publishers that their texts with minor revisions or even no change at all will address the new curricula.

The most serious and unfair result of such interregnum is that the predictable failures resulting will always be blamed on you and your cohorts as classroom teachers.[17]

---

[17] It is interesting to note that the innovations of the so-called New Math period of the 1950s and 1960s took a quite different approach from that of the Core Curriculum. University mathematicians wrote textbooks that implemented their ideas.

Letter Eight: Organizing Instruction

> *Some story books tell us of stupid, ignorant and mean teachers;*
> *but you have never read of a well-educated, intelligent,*
> *guileless young man, with the best of intentions,*
> *having the whole works tumble down about him*
> *and scurrying away like a whipped dog*
> *— all because he was not shrewd enough*
> *to cope successfully with ordinary social situations.*
> —George Miller

I note at the beginning of this chapter that this is an area that is best addressed in two ways that I will not be able to offer. First, hopefully you had in your progress through school and college some excellent teachers. You should model the organization of your instruction of some of what you experienced in those classes. Second, this is an area that is well taught in good teaching methods classes. There the opportunity to develop well-designed individual lessons to be critiqued not only by your instructor but by your peers as well provides you with opportunities to develop good classroom organization. The setting may be artificial but this aspect of instruction can be improved in that setting.

Unfortunately, too often beginning teachers retreat from those models or missed them altogether to fit their instruction into a basic pattern that too often is found in our schools. And that classroom instruction is of extremely low quality. Based on discussions with other teachers and my own observations, I assert that most class sessions across the country follow this general pattern:

1. Three-fourths or more of the time is spent reviewing the homework assignment from the previous day.
2. In five to ten minutes the teacher discusses the reading and exercises to be performed for the next class session.
3. The minute or two remaining is taken up having the students copy the assignment for the next class.

I urge you to think about those class sessions. How much time is spent teaching new concepts? Less than a quarter of the class time.

Yes, but the reading assignment will cover concept development. The text will explain what is going on. Both of those statements are probably true, but who among your students will ever read those assignments? Even the best students adopt the text-as-exercise-set approach these teachers have used in class by their own demonstration. Rarely do students read with care — to say nothing of study — their textbook; instead they simply turn to the assigned written exercises.[18]

And what about that review time? In some classes students write out exercises on the board, but that usually devolves into individual tutoring rather than class instruction.

Surely you can do better, but you need to think seriously as you organize your work.

---

[18] It was not until I was a graduate student studying statistics that I received instruction in how to study a textbook. Our instructor, Professor Morey Wantman, spent much of our initial class session going through our first text assignment sentence by sentence showing us how to raise and answer our own questions about what was being said, questions like: "What does the writer mean here?" "What does this equation tell us?" I consider that one class the most profitable of my entire education. I later learned that Professor Wantman had contributed significantly to projects that helped win World War II.

Instructional Style

With regard to how you teach, you have some serious choices to make. You have very likely come through a college program and student teaching that stressed a particular approach to instruction. (They may, in fact, even introduce you to two quite different approaches: one in your college course and another in your mentor's classroom.) Such approaches range across a spectrum usually designated by a focus on *content* and a focus on *process*. The main proponents of the *process* or *discovery* approach today are Stanford Professors Jo Boaler and Carol Dweck: the national Core Curriculum reflects some of their ideas. At the opposite extreme are more conservative approaches often designated *content*.

You have certainly been exposed to an extreme content approach in your college courses where lectures offer a take-it-or-leave-it presentation of content. The high school classrooms in which you studied very likely leaned toward content presentation, but in less extreme fashion than those college courses. Instruction that focuses on process seeks to involve the student in developing the concepts to be learned. In this approach the teacher sets the stage for the student to "discover" new ideas or to otherwise be involved with their development.

There is an even greater dichotomy in lesson presentation styles. At one extreme are those school districts that provide teachers with scripts for each day's instruction. The teacher is then expected to follow those scripts with little or no variation as do actors in stage plays. At the opposite extreme are the educational anarchists exemplified by writers like Jonathan Kozol[19] and films like *Freedom Writers*. Their approach is to throw out any established curriculum and start afresh. In some settings and for some school subjects this approach may

---

[19] See for example his personal narrative, *Death at an Early Age*.

work but it creates a serious problem for courses in which content is cumulative. In mathematics, for example, you need to master addition to learn multiplication, arithmetic to learn algebra, algebra to learn calculus. Throwing out or disrupting prerequisites has consequences up the line.[20]

Where does this leave you? You need now to make your own choice and to implement that choice. The easiest of those choices – and the one made by almost all beginning teachers – is to teach the way you were taught in your own pre-college classrooms.

Ray Patenaude's experience provides some useful insights into these concerns:

> In college and in my methods class in particular my instructors told us that teaching procedures and recipes did little to help students truly "understand." We should design teaching "experiments" and set up "discovery" activities to encourage students to create their own concepts. Also encouraged was introducing materials from other disciplines in our classrooms. In order to be good teachers, we needed to include all of this in our teaching.
>
> So I set out as a beginner to "break the mold" of traditional teaching in my classrooms. I taught discovery lessons; I included literature selections including career possibilities as well as applications. I encouraged students to consider the content I was teaching in a new light. Although I was warned by my teaching colleagues, it took me some time to realize not only how much effort went into creating those

---

[20] There is a different aspect of this lack of prerequisites that you will face. Many students will come to your classes with poor background for the topics you wish to teach. Instead of blaming teachers of lower grades, you need to find ways to address this ever-present problem. Remember that, no matter how much you wish that they did so, it is a rare student who will retain 100% of what you teach in your own classes. Thus you too will be blamed by the teachers who follow you.

lessons but, even more important, how much class time they consumed.

Finally I learned that I would be evaluated solely on my students' work on standardized examinations. If my exam scores were not up to the standards my administrators expected, I would no longer be allowed to teach college preparatory classes. I was teaching in New York State where the Regents examinations played the same kind of role that the Core Curriculum exams play. My teaching was measured by my students' success in their various courses on these single final exams, no matter what other benefits they attained from my instruction.

In fact the student achievement on the Regents exam in one of my classes did not satisfy my administrators. After my first year of teaching my eleventh grade mainstream course assignment was replaced by a remedial course.

Because my pride suffered and because I wanted to regain that class in my schedule, I completely reversed direction. I changed from the methods encouraged in college to a tight focus on the Regents curriculum and in particular on the exams based on that curriculum. My lessons, homework, quiz and test items were all modeled on examination exercises. I did few projects or discovery lessons. My class time not spent on test material was devoted to organizing and conceptualizing how the concepts related to each other in order to make recall easier for the students on the day of final exams. (In retrospect I realize that at least these latter exercises did develop connections between concepts.)

I became quite good at this conservative teaching style. In my other college preparatory courses I achieved a higher passing rate and average student grades than most of my colleagues. As a result I regained my favored teaching assignment.

Whenever I was questioned about this approach, I replied

that I was teaching what the curriculum emphasized and that it was my responsibility to ensure that what I taught adequately prepared students for academic success. (One exception to this was my care to connect earlier course concepts to more advanced concepts, as this would help me when I would see these students in my courses in later years.)

I continued this method of teaching — aligning my lessons and homework with quizzes and tests; however, as I became both more competent, proficient and self-reliant, I no longer limited my teaching to that narrow approach. Recognizing the power of discovery and investigative lessons, especially in this age of technology in which these can be done efficiently and without extra materials, I began again to incorporate those activities in my instructional program. At first I did so only occasionally, usually between content units. Over time I increased the number of these lessons. I was careful, however, to include only those that would tie closely to the ideas being introduced. It took me five years finally to accomplish this transition.

The activities included "real world" and internetbased activities that ask students to develop a model for a given situation, then answer "prediction" questions based on their model.

My experience with students and parents has convinced me that I am now good at my job. Students say that they understand the concepts I present, that they are comfortable in my classrooms and that I make content easy for them to learn.

I urge you to think about my experience as you plan your activities as a beginning teacher. It is important as you do so that you do not think that I consider my early teaching style wrong. You can see that I have returned to many of those activities over time. However, I had to accommodate to the real world of the schools in which I taught. And that real world was shaped – many would say misshaped – by those exams. Only when I had proved to my administrators — and

to myself in the process — that I could measure up to their requirements, could I expand upon their narrow view of education.

There are many lessons to be taken from that story, so well told by a master teacher. To me the most important one is that compromising with school demands may be necessary but in the end you should not lose sight of the goals you personally wish to achieve with your students.

Planning

As a beginning teacher, you cannot plan enough.

Unfortunately, most schools require plans that focus on such things as goals or objectives. While objectives are certainly important, they are usually tightly bound up with the things you do in your classroom. What you really need to provide yourself are the activities themselves. Identifying good examples to work from is far more important than deciding that you want to "have students learn the salient features of Lincoln's second inaugural address." It would be far more useful for you to note some of the particular features you wish to have addressed.

I don't want to get you into trouble here as you must give your supervisors what they require, but you also need to give yourself the nitty-gritty activities that will carry you through each class. What you don't want is to get yourself in a bind by making up an example on the spot and having it lead to a dead end.

I once watched a teacher do exactly this. He set out to show his students how to factor with the example, $x^2 - 9x - 14$, an exercise that unfortunately does not factor. When he realized that he wanted that second minus to be a plus and changed it, a student got a laugh from his classmates (and me) by asking if they could do that on the next test.

Following Up Teachable Moments

The true mark of a master teacher is the ability to make use of student contributions, especially when those contributions open unexpected lines of activity. A student question or a student error can take your class in a new and unexpected direction if you are willing to take advantage of the opportunity.

Managing this kind of thing flies in the face of your careful planning but the outcome can often be more profitable than the lesson you had planned and it can encourage your students to broaden their scope as well.

Here are some suggestions that may help you to break out of that deadly routine I described earlier:

Bell Work

Many thoughtful teachers use what is most often called "bell work" or "eye openers", start-up activities that get their students' attention focused. One of the finest with whom I ever served, junior high school teacher Iris Carl of Norwalk, Connecticut,[21] was superb at this. At the end of each class she assigned three students to "present" individual key exercises from the homework at the beginning of the following class. Then in that class,

---

[21] I am proud to have encouraged Iris to attend a meeting of the National Council of Teachers of Mathematics. She not only attended but went on to become its president, the first African American woman to serve in that role.

while those students were writing out on the board their assigned demonstrations, the rest of the class worked on a single exercise five-minute quiz. Iris would then quickly collect the quizzes, refer students to the board work, answer related questions, and move on to new work. This approach reduced her time spent on reviewing homework from three-fourths of her classes to one-fourth.

Many teachers use a modification of this kind of approach. Raoul Amstelveen, for example, has a problem for the day posted on an overhead projector or document reader that is associated with the work he will be discussing in class. His students know that they are to work on the activity as soon as they arrive in his classroom.

In many ways the first few minutes of your class are the most important. This kind of bell work gets your students focused on the day's activities and can save you five or ten minutes of instructional time.

Introducing New Work

Too much content is presented as: here it is, take it or leave it. That is, of course, very far from the way it was developed and is also a questionable way to present it. That approach directly involves only one person: the person delivering the content. Others are at best passive receivers.

Why not begin, "Here is what we want to be able to do. How do you think we might accomplish this?" I am not talking here about a discovery lesson as those lessons are designed to give each student a personal "Aha" or "I see" experience. It is quite different for a class to participate in learning about a new concept.

The first time you try this approach you may well simply receive blank stares or force many students to examine their shoes to avoid the possibility they might be called on. The reason: few of us are willing to step forward in a group setting.

Another possibility is that you will get an immediate response from an attention-seeking student that is completely off the mark.

But you know the path along which you wish to go to answer your question so you can steer your class by asking "involving" questions, some very simple if your students are not responding at all – "Could we try this?" – but some hopefully allowing for larger steps along your route – "We're stuck here. Any suggestions?" or "Is there anything wrong with that approach?" There is an art to this kind of questioning that you should seek to develop.

Beware, however, of doing too much leading. If you find that all your questions have "yes" or "no" answers, you might as well be asking your students to provide periods at the end of your sentences. You may need some of these questions to help weak students but don't fall into this trap. The difference between guided discovery and leading by the nose should be apparent.

Ray Patenaude extends his commentary here:

> I described earlier how I adopted a conservative approach to instruction in order to meet my administrators' expectations. Here is an example of my typical class day:
>
> I start with a warm-up: three SAT tune-up exercises (my school requires students to take this test); a brief review of yesterday's ideas (I'll give a few homework answers, but ask students to tell me if they need problems worked out); a daily quiz (3 to 5 exercises from previous homework assignments (my school allows only 10% of a grade to be determined by homework, so I quiz daily to make students accountable for material we've covered); a brief introduction to a topic. I then have students work in

pairs on a problem set while I grade quizzes; after which I usually give an answer or two on the day's assignment and let students ask me questions about problems, which I work out with them. During this time I can observe what areas are giving students difficulty. This allows me to revisit these areas in our next session. We usually end class with a discussion — sometimes about the current content, but often informal conversation about what's coming up in students' lives, as I'm a big believer in community in my classes.

That class has some of the elements of the bad example I offered at the beginning of this chapter, but its fast moving, activity-packed character differentiates it from that sterile approach. Control of time plays a major role in classrooms and it requires serious self-discipline to carry it off.

The Best-Laid Plans

Once again I remind you of Robert Burns' "The best laid schemes o' mice an' men, Gang aft agley." You may find yourself repeating that comment many times during your teaching career. Indeed, your well-planned lesson may not work.

My esteemed colleague Betty Krist tells two stories about her experiences working with gifted students that speak to this. In one episode she wanted to teach students how to edit a computer program. She designed a program with a number of errors that she planned to have her class seek out and correct.

Arriving a few minutes before the class was to begin she immediately found herself busy working with a student so she asked another student to copy the steps into the class demonstration computer.

But when Betty came to the point in class when she wanted to show this program that needed to be corrected, the program ran perfectly. At a loss she turned to the student who had copied the steps. His response, "I noticed that there were some errors in the program so I fixed them." So much for that lesson.

In the other class she spent over an hour working out a discovery lesson. She prepared worksheets for the students and had them organize into groups to work on the problem she had set. "By the time I had the sheets passed out," she told me, "the students had figured out what I was trying to have them accomplish. They did in a minute or two what I expected them to work out in a full class period."

A more standard form of this is the irrepressible student in a regular class who offers immediate, often wildly off base but sometimes on target, answers to questions you want your class to consider. You will need to work with this student individually to have him (it is most often a boy) participate rather than control your class.

In any case your best response to these kinds of failures may be to review them as funny stories with your students – "You really got me that time." – and your colleagues – "Did they ever mess up that lesson." The real world of your classroom will never be as predetermined as your training might lead you to believe and a sense of humor will carry you far in your teaching.

You will, however, still need to turn your class back on track in order to move on. Here is where you need to be able to wing it and revise your activities on the fly.

Raul Amstelveen brings his own perspective to classroom organization:

Bring your personality into the classroom. If you like working with your hands and do projects, by all means do that with students. Yes, students love to get out of their seats and do math! I had competitions in my informal geometry class to see which team could build the tallest building using straws. You could then bring up the use of triangles to build strength in structures. Make sure, though, that this kind of classroom is carefully managed because it can easily get out of control.

If you are a story teller or enjoy history, talk to students about controversies in mathematics and the biography of mathematicians. Remember, good teachers are passionate about their teaching and are lifelong learners.

When you get students who influence others on your side because they respect you and know that you care about them, the rest will follow.

Letter Nine: Classroom Testing

> *Testing leads to failure
> and failure leads to understanding.*
> -Burt Rutan

One of the most challenging tasks you must address is evaluating your students' achievement. Be prepared, because the first test you administer may prove deeply disheartening.

The scenario goes something like this. You teach a unit, working hard to communicate the basic concepts, drilling your students to see that they have the ideas fixed, assigning homework lessons that further ingrain the procedures that you are trying to convey. You then construct what you consider a fair test of these same ideas. Some of the questions may even repeat those you have used as illustrations in class or as homework exercises.

Two things happen. First, when you administer your very fair test, things go badly. Some students rush through it, finishing long before the time is up. For the rest of the period they irritate you and their classmates. Meanwhile, other students are unable to finish the test in the time you have allotted.

And as if that isn't bad enough, after this discouraging episode you sit down to correct the tests only to find the student achievement far below what you had expected. Your students have found every possible way to misunderstand what you have asked. Some students even miss the "give away" questions that you have included at the beginning of your test to encourage them.

You feel betrayed. Nothing has prepared you for this and you question your ability as a teacher.

As I said at the outset, be prepared for this as it happens to us all, experienced teachers as well as beginners. At least you are now forewarned.

Rethink Testing

Before I offer some specific suggestions to address these problems, I invite you to think about testing in general.

First, what does it mean when you get, say, a score of 83 on a 100-point test? One thing that it does mean is that you are a B student or a C student, depending on your local grading system. But does it also mean that you are an average student?

It probably means that you got five out of six correct answers. Was that wrong answer due to a silly error – you wrote 5267 when you meant to write 5257? You knew that it was Jefferson who said that but you spelled his name incorrectly. Or was it a complete misconception? In fact, were your five correct answers all based on the right concepts? You might have guessed "False" to a True-False question and answered correctly with no understanding whatsoever.

Consider this another way. Here in New York our state tests (those so-called Regents exams) have a passing grade of 65. Many schools use that same grade as a pass-fail cut-off.

But cross the Niagara River into Canada and their schools set 50 as their passing grade. Does that mean that Canadian school students are held to a lower standard than ours? My observation is exactly the opposite. I have worked with Canadian teachers and seen some of their curricula and the exams that test their students. My conclusion is that many of their students are superior to ours and that their tests are simply more challenging.

We teachers love numbers, even those of us who teach English and history, and we assign too much value to the numbers we come up with when grading our students. Is Gretchen a better student than Carolyn because

Gretchen's yearlong test average is 95 while Carolyn's is only 94? (Gretchen's average could even have been rounded up on a spreadsheet from 94.5 while Carolyn's was rounded down from 94.4.)

Please be sure you don't overplay what I have said here. Despite the serious problems associated with using them, these numbers are necessary. The alternative is subjective judgment and I urge you not to go there. Subjective evaluation — "I know good students from poor ones" — is strewn with pitfalls. Are you evaluating achievement or behavior? How are you going to defend your evaluations when students, administrators and parents question them?

You will far better serve your students if you simply help them to become better test takers.

Suggestions

As I hope I have made clear, just about every teacher has the kind of testing problems I have outlined. My worst came in my first year of teaching. To my chagrin, one of my better geometry students failed the final exam. He had to cancel a scout trip to the Philmont Scout Camp in New Mexico in order to retake the course that summer. You can imagine how I felt when that happened.

Here then are four points you should consider about testing:

1. At the beginning of any course students are unprepared

for the format you will be using for your tests. You can address this by assigning them a practice test for homework and, once they have worked the exercises, reviewing with them how they should approach the similar quiz you will offer. This may seem like a waste of class time, but I promise you that it will give your students a better opportunity to demonstrate what they know. Don't expect anything to completely address your students' test-taking anxiety, but this should help many of them.

Then you'll need to work individually with some. I had one fine student who broke out in hives whenever she faced a class test. It took work with a guidance counselor, the student's parents and finally a medical doctor to respond to her very real difficulties. We worked out a program of decreasing sedation through which she finally adjusted at least partly to her anxieties.

2. To address the problems of classroom administration of your tests, I suggest that you occasionally use a quite different scoring method.

Suppose, say, you have made up ten test questions of increasing difficulty. Instead of scoring them ten points apiece, score them on the total number of correct answers according some form of the following scheme:

correct	score
10	100
9	95
8	90
7	85
6	80
5	70
4	60
3	50
2	40
1	20
0	0

In other words, the first two correct answers count 20 each, the next four 10 each and the final four 5 each. This has nothing to do with which questions are answered correctly. If, for example, a student gives correct answers to questions 1, 2, 4, 5, 7 and 8, the student's test score would be 80, not the 60 that 6 of 10 correct answers would normally score.

This kind of scoring has three major advantages. First, it allows your weaker students to achieve reasonable grades. This is especially true of students who work slowly. I once had a very bright student who never finished a test, but he always answered every question he attempted correctly.

(He was occasionally late for class as well because he even walked slowly.)

Equally important or perhaps even more important, this scoring allows you to include difficult questions on your test. This gives the test another advantage: you are able to challenge your better students.

Also, you can make at least one question difficult or time consuming enough that all students will be hard pressed to finish the test in the time period allotted. That way you can avoid the discipline problems that arise when students finish early.

3. Factoring grades comes hard to many teachers. "If he got a 60, he deserves a 60," is a common mantra. But that flies in the face of what I described at the beginning of this letter. A 60 on a specific test certainly does not mean that a student knows exactly three-fifths of the content you have taught.

    Suppose you have given a test on which your class average is 60 and, upon reviewing what you asked, you feel that a more reasonable average would be 80. A computer spreadsheet will allow you to make this class-wide adjustment quickly and easily.

4. One of your toughest problems remains that of challenging your better students while you support those of less ability.

By posting and describing interesting bonus problems you can often capture the attention of your best students. Better to have them working on a challenging exercise than surreptitiously getting into trouble as you address more mundane topics.

Telling individual students that you think that they are capable of addressing specific problems can get them started and you can monitor their progress, giving hints if you feel that is appropriate.

5.   Some teachers find it a good policy to allow one test grade per semester to be set aside. Carefully handled, this can give your students a chance to overcome the negative effects of a very poor test grade.

Testing is an important aspect of teaching. It serves many purposes in addition to evaluating your students' progress. For example, it can suggest where you need to focus more attention in your teaching. Used wisely testing can play a very important role in your instructional program.

Letter Ten: Standardized Tests

> *The one size fits all approach*
> *to standardized testing*
> *is convenient but lazy.*
> —James Dyson

Among the crosses you must be prepared to bear as a classroom teacher are standardized tests. I speak here of the commercially constructed tests designed to measure your students and you against other students and teachers regionally, statewide, nationally or even internationally.[22]

I have serious reservations about these exams, but they are increasingly a fact of life for all teachers today even in the primary grades. As they will be administered in your classroom, you must recognize the time lost to instruction in your long-term planning. And because they carry both rewards and penalties to your students and you, you should consider them seriously.

No matter what their attitude toward these tests, most teachers simply live with them and that is, I believe, the best option open to you, especially as a beginning teacher. I suggest, however, that you should help your students (and indirectly yourself) by communicating to them some common sense test-taking skills.

---

[22] I write this at a time when we have a national revolt by teachers as well as students and their parents against the number of standardized tests being administered in our schools and the purposes to which they are being assigned. You may have strong feelings about this, but as a beginning teacher you should think seriously before getting involved in such a politically charged issue.

Today we have an entire industry devoted to developing these tests. If you teach in a wealthy suburb, many of your students will be enrolled outside of school in Kaplan, Princeton or other test prep programs, mostly designed to help them score high on college entrance exams, the so-called college boards. Those programs do not focus on content but rather on test-taking skills. And they work! Of course this does not mean that they necessarily improve their clients' knowledge but only that they improve their scores. And scores count today: in fact they can define students' futures, because college admission and scholarships are associated with high scores.

Okay, then what can you do to help your students? Almost exclusively, these tests involve multiple-choice questions — or, facetiously, multiple-guess items. Unsophisticated students simply read the question (the so-called stem) and, if they don't know the answer, move on to the next question.[23] They don't think, for example, one of the simplest skills of all: testing each of the choices against the stem, in that way eliminating wrong answers and zeroing in on the correct one.

There are dozens of similar test-taking tricks that you can find on the Web by googling "test taking tips." But telling your students about these techniques is not enough. Include some multiple choice items on your class tests and discuss these methods when you review their answers with them.

In New York State schools where the state Regents examinations are administered, teachers joke about reviewing for those exams. "The first week of school, you teach with a regular text; the rest of the year you use the Regents review book." While that is an exaggeration, in

---

[23] Even skipping questions causes problems. Some students then get out of sequence, placing answers in the wrong places on machine-scoring sheets. You will do well to warn them about this at the time they take such a test.

most schools the final month or so of the school year is devoted to review for those exams. Old tests are assigned and instruction focuses on types of items that have appeared on the tests most often.

While there are obvious aspects of this that are open to criticism, my own experience as a student was that I strongly reinforced my understanding of the content we had previously covered during that final review.[24] This is indeed appropriately called "teaching to the test," but it did more than that for me.

There is, in fact, psychological support for this end-of-theyear time set aside for review and re-teaching. Psychologists tell us that review reinforces understanding better when that recapitulation is separated in time from the original instruction.

I am not suggesting that you devote a major share of your instructional time to administer and review practice items from the standardized tests your students will take. Rather, I encourage you to include those tests in your thinking about your assignments and classroom activities throughout the school year.

Finally, I add a few words about helping your students study for a test. I suggest that you need first to assess your own test prep habits. Mine are dreadful. For example, I go back to notes I have taken and find that they are illegible. (My father, whose own handwriting could have won calligraphic prizes, once offered this mild criticism, "You know, Gerry, you have quite attractive handwriting, but in what language is it written?")

I have already suggested offering a practice test to help your students understand the kind of questions you will be

---

[24] In one embarrassing episode when I was a student my football coach asked me, "Is it true you got a perfect score on the solid geometry regents?" I was delighted to respond that it was, but I was less pleased when he walked away shaking his head. I could see that he was having difficulty associating my achievement in the classroom with my failures on the athletic field.

asking, but this also helps them focus on key ideas. Students should also review their returned homework papers and the related textual content. You can stress the main formulas to be remembered. Those suggestions are not meant to be all inclusive; you can, for example, find many others on the web. You can also do your students a favor by having a class discussion of how each of them plans to prepare. This gets them thinking about study habits and hopefully a few of them will offer good suggestions.

I conclude these comments with an example of a review technique I employed that failed utterly. In preparing my students for the geometry Regents exam, I carefully wrote out on the chalkboard a theorem proof that contained a number of serious errors. We used that error-infested proof in class to root out those mistakes. As it happened, that very proof was requested on that year's exam and I thought that my students would be well prepared to supply it.

I was dead wrong. Unfortunately, many of the students made exactly those errors they were supposed to avoid. I suspect that they had dutifully copied that proof into their notebooks in the form I originally gave them in class without the corrections and they subsequently accepted it in that form in their review for the test.

Letter Eleven: Your Classroom

> *Photographs cannot show models in their full splendor.*
> *The most complicated are not only difficult to make*
> *but are highly decorative: a perfect instance*
> *of the connection between truth and beauty.*
> —H. S. M. Coxeter

I should note at the outset that you should consider yourself fortunate if you are assigned a classroom of your own. Too many beginners are "roller-skate teachers," that is, they have to race from classroom to classroom to teach, their materials stuffed into briefcases or mounted on wheeled carts.

I recall my own years as a roller-skate teacher, rushing into a classroom to write something on the chalkboard only to find all the boards completely filled with writing and with the underscored word <u>Save</u> written at the top. Later, as technology advanced, I entered a similar classroom planning to write on an overhead projector only to find the entire acetate roll filled and in the same way marked for retention.

I finally responded in kind to those selfish — or at least thoughtless — teachers. In each case I invited a student to erase material to clear enough space for me to write what I needed. That way, when the angry teacher complained to me about my "erasure of important material," I could honestly say that (1) I did not erase that material, but (2) I appreciated the fact that some space was created for me to carry on with my own lesson. As I look back on those responses, I am less comfortable with them, but they did accomplish my purpose: from then on at least some space was left for me.

Let's say then that you do have a room assigned as yours. That will almost always mean that you will have a group of homeroom students, students you may or may not see for the rest of the day. As far as the school is concerned, your responsibility for those students goes little farther than taking attendance and occasionally marching them to assemblies and seating them together there.

In any case, your relationship with those students is different from that in your courses. I always considered my homeroom groups a kind of family. And in one school this was reinforced by having those homeroom groups stay together with the same teacher through all four years of high school and associating you with their class activities.

Since I didn't have the kind of confrontational relationship with these students that I had as an instructor, I tried to serve them individually and collectively as their informal counselor. For example, after the first 10-week marking period each year I divided the group into teams to compete to see which team would increase their grades the most in the next semesters. Their response to this and other attention I gave them was very positive and I am always invited back for their five-year reunions.

Making Your Classroom Attractive

There is a sterile institutional atmosphere that pervades an undecorated school classroom. It is the same kind of atmosphere you find when you visit a house empty of its furnishings. You can change this atmosphere with help from your students.

If, like me, you are all thumbs at designing decorations, do what I always did whenever I moved to a new school: visit the school's art teacher. You will find them a wonderful source for decorating ideas you would never think of and, if you have ideas of your own, they will enhance them. In many schools today there will be a bonus to this contact. With schools playing down all subjects except math and language arts, art and music teachers feel especially isolated and threatened. By simply asking art teachers for help, you will almost assuredly gain new friends, friends you will respect for their contributions.

What you and your students design to make your room more livable will depend, of course, on the subject you teach. Here, for example, teachers of foreign languages and teachers of world history have a real advantage. You can visit any local travel agency to obtain posters for countries around the world.

Math teachers can have students construct polyhedron models that custodians can help you hang from the ceiling of your classroom.[25] One school in which I served had a six-foot model of a slide rule. I hung it above one of the chalkboards. In almost every class I taught from seventh graders to seniors, sooner or later a student would ask what "that contraption" was. That gave me a nice opportunity to connect adding powers to addition on a logarithmic scale. In advanced classes this also enhanced the connection with those strange *log* and *ln* keys on their calculators.

Something math and history teachers can share are number lines running around the room walls above the writing areas. Of course the math line will illustrate positive and negative numbers and have distinctive places for special numbers like π, e and various roots, while the historical number line will feature dates of significant events.

---

[25] There is a wonderful source for polyhedron patterns, a book titled simply and appropriately *Polyhedron Models*. It has everything from the tetrahedron to the quasitruncated cuboctrahedron and the stellated icosi-dodecahedron. The book represents a lifetime of preparation by a cloistered Benedictine monk, Father Magnus Wenninger.

Teachers of all subjects can find photos or paintings of significant contributors to their field. For science classes in particular important laws and advances can be personalized by such pictures. I will forever associate Einstein's discoveries with the photo of him with his tongue out.

One suggestion. Whenever possible choose an attractive portrayal of the person illustrated. Far better, for example, would be Charles Darwin as a young man ready to sail on the Beagle than the usual depiction of him as a full-bearded, sickly old man.

Seating Arrangements

Teachers employ a variety of patterns for the student desks in their classrooms. The most conservative and formal pattern is by rows and columns. That has always been my preference. Some teachers like Ray Patenaude prefer desks in pairs; others, desks in groups of four;[26] and, of course, some teachers arrange the seats in a semicircle or circle.

I urge you to think seriously about how you arrange your desks. Whatever arrangement you use, align the seats each day in an orderly fashion, as this will convey one more sense of discipline. Granted that this will seem a minor issue but, like your wearing appropriate clothing, it will represent you as a disciplined model. And remember, today students in our disorderly world need such order wherever they can find it.

Problem of the Week

---

[26] William Bailey, one of my doctoral students, experimented with students working in teams of four with very positive results.

As a math teacher, I found it useful to post a general *Problem of the Week* on my homeroom bulletin board. This attracted the attention of many students including several I did not expect would have any interest in such problems. I tried to make these exercises challenging but not closely aligned with particular content. This gave younger students an equal footing with their more advanced classmates. The problems were often taken home to involve and challenge parents. These exercises ranged from old chestnuts, problems that had been around for many years, to new ones I came across in my recent reading. Here is one of those old chestnuts:

You have 12 coins, one of which is counterfeit and you seek to identify the false coin by using three weighings on a two-pan balance.[27] (a) If you know that the false coin is lighter, how can you accomplish this? (b) If you only know that the coin differs from the others (it could be lighter or heavier) how should you proceed?

The same kind of thing can be done in other fields. Here, for example, is one that might be used in an English or social studies class:

Hopefully all of us are familiar with Patrick Henry's famous revolutionary call to arms, "Give me liberty or give me death!" Find three other memorable statements by Henry, at least one of which does not relate to the Revolutionary War.

And here is one for the science classroom:

Many of science's basic concepts are set out in groups of three laws. Name four of these groups and give the three laws for one of them.

You will serve yourself well if you post such problems and then take class time to discuss them. And you will also assist your memory by keeping a file of problems and demonstrations.

---

[27] A two-pan balance is like a seesaw. It offers just two possibilities: If the weights are equal on the two pans, they balance; if they differ, the pan with the heavier weight goes down.

Letter Twelve: Technology

> *My first question is: what is the educational need and how could technology address this better than the current approach? Otherwise, I won't waste everyone's time.*
> –Peter Rowlett

New tools are being added to teachers' armamentarium almost daily but we are a long way from a time when you will be replaced by a computer or robot.

As a teacher you should constantly keep in mind that you are the major driving force supporting the academic progress of your students. All the books and computers and electronic apps and projectors and white boards and recorders and other paraphernalia serve only as bells and whistles in support of your instruction.

Don't misunderstand my point. Those tools can play important roles in your teaching, but you are still needed as the orchestra conductor. President Garfield made this point when he described the finest education as the famous 19th century teacher "Mark Hopkins on one end of a log and a student on the other." No intervention was necessary to enhance that communication.

In fact some of these tools make teaching even more difficult. They offer easy access to distracting activities, they increase the opportunities for some students to surreptitiously communicate among themselves as you try to teach, their games are addictive and even loss and theft of these expensive devices become problems. In this regard they represent additional burdens you must bear.

Hopefully you will have met many technological tools before you enter your classroom. And you must determine what particular tools will be available to your individual students. For example, will your students have access to computers in your classes and, if so, will they also have access to them at home? You cannot plan to post homework assignments on a website if some of your students cannot monitor that website.

In my own teaching I have classified technology in two categories: (1) necessary and (2) supplemental.

First among the tools I consider necessary are those that support your communication. In our earliest schools students used slates and teachers wrote on chalkboards to share written activities. Today chalkboards are still around (although they are almost always enhanced in various ways) and overhead projectors and document readers play similar basic roles. Of course, textbooks fit this category as well.

All the rest I consider supplemental.[28] That does not mean, however, that such tools cannot support your instruction.

Primary among the supplemental tools are computing devices that support word processors. These allow students to write reports and answer homework questions. Of almost equal value are spreadsheets that can be used to organize and present information.

Calculation devices that carry out computations, evaluate functions and display graphs are useful not just in math classes but in all fields. Physics and chemistry classes are especially well served by them. And remarkably these devices have become increasingly inexpensive.

Whatever your feelings about technology, these devices

---

[28] An exception may be a calculator required for one of the state or national examinations.

are available both in schools and in homes and you need to accommodate your instructional program and your own thinking about teaching to them. Here are some of the things you should consider in this regard:

1. You must watch for concepts skipped over when you use technological tools. Are spell checkers and grammar helpers allowing students to bypass basic writing concepts? Are calculators substituting for thinking about mathematical operations?

2. Instructional time is extremely important. You will find that there is a great deal of content to communicate in the courses you teach. And some computing devices and computer software require much instructional time to familiarize students with their use. Are the positive values of those instructional enhancements worth the time you must devote to teaching their use?

PERSONAL

Letter Thirteen: The Quality of the Subject You Teach

> *A teacher can never truly teach*
> *unless he is still learning himself.*
> *A lamp can never light another lamp*
> *unless it continues to burn its own flame.*
> *The teacher who has come to the end of his subject,*
> *who has no living traffic with his knowledge*
> *but merely repeats his lessons to his students,*
> *can only load their minds; he cannot quicken them.*
> --Rabindranath Tagore

Sadly, I believe that many school classroom teachers do not respect the content they are teaching. Are you now or will you be one of those?

Your experience in college has encouraged this lack of respect. You have studied more advanced content or addressed content in more sophisticated ways and those studies have made your school content seem trivial.

This is very unfortunate because failure to respect the content you are teaching can make your classroom instruction more like a job than a profession.

I urge you to find ways to assure yourself that what you are teaching is honorable and significant in its own right. It is not just "baby stuff" and that applies, I believe, to what you are teaching in kindergarten just as much as it applies to what you seek to convey in high school chemistry.

Here you will have to look to your own experience to find aspects of what you will teach to reinforce your respect of your subject.

In my case I can identify a number of my own school experiences that I continue to consider life-enhancing. One of those was diagramming sentences in English classes, an activity that most of my classmates hated but that gave me a logical connection with writing that continues to affect my thinking. Another seemingly trivial example was a unit in junior high school in which we studied mythology, meeting characters like Zeus and Athena and their associated stories. Although no connection was offered by my teachers, that experience has affected my attitude toward religion ever since.

I will illustrate my point here with an example from mathematics that I have used to convince not only teachers but the general public that there are challenging mathematical problems at every level.

Here is a simple obtuse triangle. Draw a segment or segments to divide its interior into acute triangles.

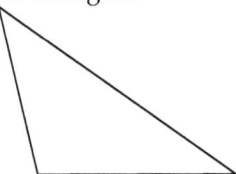

All you need to know to understand that problem is what are acute and obtuse angles, acute and obtuse triangles. Those are definitions known to third or fourth grade students. I expect, however, that most of you reading this, including math teachers, will be challenged by it.

For over sixty years that problem has served to remind me that mathematics can be made challenging at any level. I urge you to seek out examples from your own field that impress and encourage you.

Your Projects and Activities File

I recommended in an earlier letter that you keep a problem and activities file and I repeat that recommendation here. If you are like me, you not only forget good activities but even for those you remember you will often fail to recall key points. They end up like those jokes people tell that get twisted in the telling and draw only groans from their audience. Good notes can address these problems.

Art DiVito suggests a modification of this. Keep a file of the mistakes your students make on quizzes. You'll identify, he claims, a ton of them and he only regrets that he did not do this himself. Start early, he suggests, and you'll accumulate enough to organize into a talk, article or even book. Whether or not you use them for that purpose, a review of these errors should influence your teaching of the topics with which they are associated.

Challenge Yourself

Your teaching of is, I am convinced, enhanced by your continuing to address challenging ideas yourself. Just as you challenge your students, you should at least occasionally challenge yourself. Such activity has a real possibility of affecting your classroom instruction positively. It will remind you what it is like to find your way through unmarked country and this will give you greater appreciation for what your students have to face. It will broaden your understanding of what you are teaching. And it will provide you with examples you can use in your classes.

A Personal Experience

I close this letter with a personal experience. Early in my teaching career and late in hers, my Johnson City High School department head, Anne Courtright, posed a challenging construction problem to my colleague, Walt Scheer, and me. Mrs. Courtright was a wonderful mentor and we had so much respect for her that we each set out immediately to attack the problem.

Although her challenge seemed at first to be a reasonable exercise, I soon found it to be very difficult. And indeed Walt came up with a solution and I did not.

I was thrilled by Walt's complex solution to that exercise and I helped my geometry class to work through it as an illustration of how problems often require complex solutions.

I also added Walt's solution to my personal activities file.

That led to an interesting sequel to that story. Years later when I was writing a chapter on transformation geometry for Ray Jorgenson's high school geometry text, I thought of that problem again. I wondered if it could be solved through use of transformations, an approach at the time new to school instruction. And indeed, the problem was easily solved by an appropriate application of a transformation called a dilation.

You can only imagine the thrill that achievement gave me. Drawing on that earlier, long remembered experience, I was able to apply a new tool to solve a difficult exercise. I have rarely been so happy.

Letter Fourteen: Role Models

> *Colleagues are a wonderful thing – but mentors, that's where the real work gets done.*
> —Junot Diaz

As you think seriously about teaching mathematics, you should draw on your own experience as a student in school and college. Hopefully (but sadly not necessarily) you studied in the classrooms of some excellent teachers and you can review the features of their instruction that impressed you. You should ask yourself: What did they do right? What can I emulate in my own instruction? Are there ways they could have been still better?

I was very fortunate to have been taught by two exemplary Brighton High School teachers: Elswood Hill and Robert Collins. The main impression I gained of them as their student was their seriousness of purpose. Both were no-nonsense teachers whose expectations we students fulfilled because they simply offered no alternative.

When I later returned to teach at Brighton, these fine teachers became my colleagues and that further enhanced my opinion of them. Indeed, in my second year there, Bob Collins left teaching to become head of the school guidance program and I assumed his class schedule. He was helpful and supportive in that transition.

I was shocked, however, once I had established my own teaching reputation, to have two students ask me if they could transfer from Mr. Hill's geometry section to my own. When I inquired what was their reason, they told me they found Hill's class boring. Far from considering their request a compliment to my own teaching, I found it profoundly disturbing. My earlier experience in Hill's geometry classroom had been formative: that year had turned me on to math. In particular, Hill was a sailor[29] and he used navigation examples to illustrate some of the geometric concepts. By this and other means he made geometry an important aspect of the real world for me and my classmates.

What bothered me about the students' request was that it suggested that they considered me an entertainer rather than a teacher. That forced me to rethink my approach to teaching seriously. Was I shortchanging my students by playing to their immature sensibilities?

I took that opportunity not only to encourage those students to appreciate Hill's qualities as a teacher but also to reassess my own activities. I decided that entertaining my students was only justified in support of instruction, otherwise it subtracted from valuable instructional time and indirectly from student achievement.

Among my college teachers three stand out: Arnold Ross of Notre Dame, Arthur Danese of the University of Rochester and later the College at Fredonia and Mary Dolciani of Hunter College.

Ross had an ability I have rarely seen in a teacher (and that I have never been able to replicate) of making each student feel that his lectures were personal conversations. As he talked and wrote on an overhead projector, his eyes darted around his large classroom, stopping briefly on individual students to smile or frown.

You knew he liked you even when he turned your

---

[29] Hiil's small boat sailing served him and me as well as we both served as navigation officers during World War II.

question into a joke to share with the rest of the class. Once, for example, when I asked a question about a proof, he responded, "Perhaps because it is so small, an important exponent seems to have eluded you." I saw immediately where I had gone astray and laughed with the rest of the class.

Another instructor could have made this a serious put-down.

But he could occasionally offer more direct put-downs as well. He hated gum-chewing and — this in a graduate course! — he spoke out directly in class to an errant student, "It has been proved by experiments involving the cow that steady motion of the jaw muscle has a strong negative effect on the operation of the brain." That drew a roar of laughter and I never again saw a gum-chewer in his classroom.

Mary Dolciani was a highly honored teacher at City University of New York and the senior author of what were for many years the most popular high school math texts. I only knew Mary from a series of summer programs held in various New England states in which we taught. Away from the classroom I found her a very shy person. I recall, for example, our first meeting. I found her sitting at a table alone in a cafeteria jammed with math teachers who did not recognize her. When I asked to join her and she graciously accepted, I found her an interesting conversationalist and for an hour we shared stories of our World War II experiences.

I made it a point to attend her series of lectures based on her work with secret codes during that war. This was of special interest to me as I had been my ship's coding officer. There this shy woman became a different person. She metamorphosed into a dynamic, forceful teacher in complete command of her audience.

My favorite class of all my studies, however, was a differential equations course taught by Arthur Danese. He made those applications – cooling coffee and exploding populations – come alive. My favorite was his story about field mice left to breed and thrive without predation for a time: "If after twenty years, you were to place those mice in line nose to tail," he said, "you would have enough to stretch from here to Albany and back," and he added slyly, "with enough left over to reach eleven times to the moon."

Can Bad Teachers Serve as Models?

The answer to that question is straightforward: indeed they can. I consider myself most fortunate in having studied with those fine teachers of the previous section. Sadly, the teaching tradition, especially in mathematics, is not good and you may have passed all the way through school and college without meeting an excellent instructor. But even your bad teachers can serve as models. You can ask yourself: What was wrong with their teaching? How can I avoid their errors? And how can I be different?

Those exemplary teachers and really poor teachers are the extremes. Almost all teachers have both good and bad features and each offers you a basis for selection and rejection of characters.

One of my favorite bad teaching episodes took place in the Princeton University classroom of a well-known senior professor.[30] He was not only a fine mathematician but he was also an excellent expositor; now, however, he was lecturing to us high school teachers and he spoke of the problems we created for him on the first day of class: "I am used to teaching advanced doctoral students with much more background than you have, so I encourage you to stop me with questions at any time you do not understand

---

[30] So well known in fact that his role as a Princeton department head was portrayed in a minor role in the book and film, *A Beautiful Mind*.

a concept or need me to clarify a point. This will be a big help for me in my teaching as well." There were no questions in that first class so he repeated his invitation at the beginning of the second class.

Later that hour one of my classmates interrupted him to ask about one of the points the professor had made. The instructor's thoughtless response was, "That is too idiotic a question to deserve an answer," and he went on with his lecture.

Finally recognizing his error, the professor apologized at the beginning of the third class, but that was, as you might expect, the last hand raised in that entire course.

Think about that terrible instructional error. It was so blatant that it makes for a humorous story, but it is the kind of trap that you too can easily fall into in your classroom. It is a great temptation to embarrass a student and gain a laugh from the rest of your class in doing so. Put-downs are easy responses to questions or actions that we consider beneath us. But it takes an Arnold Ross to use them without destroying the confidence and even angering one or more students. The line between friendly banter and bullying is a narrow one.

In contrast I conclude this letter with an example of a teacher generally rated as poor — my own children later studied with her and considered her one of their worst teachers — but who was very important to me for just one incident.

I was not a good student in elementary school. My dad referred to me as his CCC student — reinterpreting the New Deal Civil Conservation Corps acronym of that time. In fifth grade this teacher called me to her desk after assigning the class the task of writing a précis of an article in *Life Magazine*. "Gerry," she said, "I think you are smarter than you do yourself. Your work is poor simply because you don't try and I want you to test yourself with this assignment. Just see if you can't do high quality work." When I agreed to try — thinking "just this once can't hurt" — she asked me how I might go about this task. She accepted my suggestions and sent me back to my seat.

The paper I produced she told me was one of the best in the class and she had me read it to my classmates, thus giving me additional recognition. (Despite that, she only assigned me a B+ and I remain convinced that I deserved an A.) But the important lesson of that episode reversed my attitude toward school: I realized that I was short-changing myself and I went on to earn significantly better grades.

I have tried in various ways to replicate that contribution with my own students and I urge you to search your own experiences as a student to draw from them similar lessons.

Letter Fifteen: What Do You Bring to Teaching?

> *Students assigned to the novice teacher over the first two years of their career lose roughly .10 standard deviations in student achievement.*
> —Douglas Staiger and Jonah Rockoff

I urge you to inventory your own skills and attitude as you become a math teacher. What do you bring to this profession? Why are you entering it? What are your positive qualities that you can build on? What are your negative qualities, aspects of your nature that you should seek either to correct or to avoid.

In doing this you should not be trying to sell yourself. If you have a teaching position, you have probably already done that; rather, you are doing this for yourself.

I wish I could offer myself as a model for anyone choosing teaching as a career, but my entrance to this field serves more as a cautionary tale than a model for preparation.

Consider the odd mix of motivations that led me to become a math teacher. Because I was editor of my college newspaper and hated dissecting animals, I drifted from an undergraduate pre-med science curriculum to become an English major. I had worked as a trainer for a local football team and as a camp counselor and I had even done some substitute teaching before graduating with a B.A. in English so I considered teaching. I saw myself as a potential Mr. Chips, modeled on the James Hilton character, and teaching at one of the major private schools.

I even entered a master's degree program in English but immediately recognized that I was in over my head. My six fellow students were far better prepared: for example, one of them, Galway Kinnell, later won the Pulitzer Prize for Poetry; another later wrote Broadways plays. I did take one thing from that punishing experience, however: I gained empathy for underachievers having been for that academic year the class "dumb kid": in that case myself.

That was when that principal of a rural Warsaw Central School called me to offer me a position teaching math. "But my background is in English," I responded. "You have enough math coursework to teach it," he told me and, eager to get out of that punishing graduate program, I accepted the position. One aspect attracted me: I would be the school's assistant football coach.

Thus my background and motivation were all wrong. Although I had enjoyed my math studies, it was not at that time my chosen field. In fact, I had little preparation for teaching any subject. I took that first job simply as an escape from that embarrassing graduate program. And its principal attraction was the associated coaching assignment. As I look back on what I brought to what would over a very short time grow into the teaching profession that has meant so much to me, I wonder that I got there at all. I was most fortunate that at the time there was a seller's market for teachers.

I did, however, take my new assignment seriously. I realized that, despite what that principal told me, my math background was far too thin. In response to this perceived deficiency, I borrowed some textbooks and undertook a personal refresher course. I went through college algebra and calculus texts to improve my background, in the process realizing how clear the concepts became and wondering why I hadn't understood them so well when I slid through those courses as a college undergraduate.

Those three months preparing myself to become a math teacher were central to all that would follow. I found that I truly loved the subject matter. It made sense to me and I wanted to study it further. So I added my newfound commitment to mathematics to my commitment to working with adolescents.

Okay, now I had the motivation. What else did I bring to teaching? I didn't inventory myself at the time, but I know my drawbacks. In particular, intellectually I am a sprinter, not a distance runner. I readily take on tasks but I am easily bored with routine. And much of teaching is routine: especially reviewing student homework and grading papers. It took me some time to learn to cope with those mundane tasks; in fact I continue to avoid or postpone them. And even now I have to discipline myself to complete tasks like writing this book.

So I was a mix as I expect you are. Knowing my positives and negatives, however, I have tried to address them and that is the value of such an inventory.

You need to think about your own qualities and shortcomings in the way I have done here. Only then can you think of ways to build on your qualities and ways to work around, to avoid or at least to reduce your shortcomings. Here are some of the questions I urge you to consider:

Why did you decide to teach?

Why did you choose your particular teaching field as your subject? Or did you?

Evaluate the reasons for those choices. Are they good or bad?

Do you consider your content preparation strong or weak?

What are the positive aspects of your personality that you bring to teaching?

What are the negatives you feel you must overcome?

What do you think you are going to like best about teaching? And worst?

You should be able to think of other questions specific to you.

But don't simply answer the questions. Apply them to your

thinking about your role as a classroom teacher. And if among them you find deficiencies, plan ways to address them.

If Your Knowledge is Deficient

Of course you should seek ways of addressing a deficiency in subject matter knowledge. This can involve personal study or enrollment in college or adult education courses. You can enroll in formal programs at a local college or join one of the many online courses offered. The advantage participation in a class offers is the opportunity to interact with your peers who will raise questions and explore avenues that you might miss. But meanwhile you have students to teach. Raul Amstelveen has an interesting perspective on this:

One of the easiest ways to lose respect among your peers and students is not to have the necessary content knowledge to teach. The best way to address a current lack of content knowledge, however, is to make sure that you are prepared for what you will teach each day. Plan exactly which problems you will use in class and on homework assignments. After you have made your selection, work all the problems yourself to make sure you know how to solve them. Assign for your students harder, more challenging problems than those you will use in exams and practice those problems beforehand as well. Especially for a beginner, it looks really bad if you try to demonstrate an exercise in class that you cannot solve.

Those suggestions apply primarily to factual or computational aspects of teaching, but they also apply to the development of class activities and discussions. Just because you want freedom in a class discussion, that does not mean that you should simply wing it. You need to think of salient points that you want your students to address. Students will enjoy directionless talk — and they love particularly stories about yourself — but, unless those stories contribute to your instructional goals, they are better left to other settings. Preparing where at least in general you wish a classroom discussion to go can turn them into effective educational experiences.

At the same time, as Art DiVito suggests, your colleagues will respect you if you seek their help and advice. For example, he cites the teaching of a topic that seems easy to address at first but that has many hidden pitfalls. An experienced colleague may well have addressed those very pitfalls and would be willing to share that background with you.

Still you are bound to make embarrassing mistakes. The best you can do is: Don't make the same mistake more than once.

Just as student mistakes can lead to learning; so too the mistakes you make in your teaching should lead you to learn. Find out what went wrong and correct it, getting assistance if necessary to do so. In fact, every lesson you teach can be improved. Always be on the lookout for ways to make these improvements. In this way you continue to grow.

Letter Sixteen: Dealing with Disappointment

*Don't dwell on what went wrong.
Instead, focus on what to do next.
Spend your energies on moving forward
toward finding the answer.*
—Denis Waitley

Although I cannot prove it, I'm sure the inability to cope with disappointment and frustration is one of the reasons so many young teachers leave the profession and some statistics suggest that as many as half of all beginners leave within the first five years of their first teaching assignment.

Ray Patenaude offers his experiences in this regard:

When I was in college, a public service ad on TV recruiting teachers touted, *Be a hero, be a teacher!* The ad highlighted the important impact that teachers have on young people's lives. Images of young teachers having positive interactions with students in classrooms, and successful students with teachers standing behind them filled the screen.

I was impressed.

Sometimes the lofty images also came from myself. My summer camp counseling experiences influenced my decision to become a teacher. I was good as a counselor and enjoyed working with kids and I assumed that I'd naturally be a good teacher — right from the start. Further contributing to my personal aspirations, the movie *Stand and Deliver* was running in theaters my last year of college. This movie was based on the true story of Jaime Escalante,

a teacher in Los Angeles who motivated and inspired his impoverished
Hispanic students, some of whom were gang members, to achieve outstanding results on Advanced Placement exams. While I realized that was a tough image to live up to, I hoped that I could aspire to such excellence.

I was excited! I was going to be a teacher, a hero. And I was going to make a difference!

Now after many years in the classroom I know that I have made a difference for my students and I know too that I made that difference from the first day I began to teach. But that only became clear to me over time. Early in my teaching tenure I often wondered if I had chosen the right career. Instead of reflecting those attractive images of honored teachers providing great service, teaching seemed to represent much very hard work for few achievements, fewer rewards and many disappointments.

Understand That You Don't Have to be Perfect

Of course, some teachers are natural showmen and women. I have known several of them and you will probably meet them among your teaching colleagues — or, if you are particularly fortunate, will have met them as your own teachers. If you are one of those fortunate students or born master teachers, be thankful, but the odds are against either possibility. And even if you have won either of those lotteries, be prepared for the frustration and disappointment that are part and parcel of classroom teaching.

Think of it this way: you must deal with dozens of students, to say nothing of the many colleagues, supervisors, administrators and parents hovering in the background. And although each student won't represent the kind of special challenge described in an earlier letter, even the so-called normal students represent unique problems.

I promise you that things will go wrong. You'll prepare a great lesson and it will flop miserably. You'll feel comfortable with a unit you have taught and the preparation you have given your students for the fair test on the material you have prepared and every student, including the best, will fall far short of your expectations. What your students knew yesterday they will have forgotten today. You'll initiate a discussion that you are sure will appeal to your students and no one will respond to your questions or their responses will lead the class in the wrong direction.

On some days nothing will work. Your students will be excited about some out-of-class activity — a big game, a field trip for another class, one of their classmates arrested — and every time you get one group settled down another will erupt in whispers or giggles.

These are the frustrations and disappointments that you must expect as a teacher. You're not alone; every teacher has temporary set-backs and bad days. You just have to learn to put up with some of them and to deal with others.

While not a comprehensive list, what follows are some suggestions for addressing the frustrations teaching presents on a regular basis.

Recognize that you will make mistakes

I recall one study focusing on teachers as decision makers stating that during instruction, planning and grading, a typical teacher will make over one hundred decisions each school day.[31] Given that number, it is guaranteed that you will make at least a few poor decisions every day. You cannot always be right. Whether it's questioning the way you taught something that led the class to more confusion instead of the clarity you envisioned, to getting a "look" from a student and wondering if you said something wrong, know this – *you will make mistakes!*

While this advice doesn't necessarily help you feel better about any particular mistake that you make, you should findsolace in the fact that you are not alone in poor decision making. Veteran teachers routinely question decisions they made in instructing, planning, and grading — they appropriately call it "reflecting" and try to figure out what they'd do better next time. You should do the same.

And as your career progresses, you will get better at decision-making. As with any skill, the more you practice, the better you will get. In *Outliers: The Story of Success*, Malcolm Gladwell tells us, "Researchers have settled on what they believe is the magic number for true expertise: ten thousand hours." Based on an eight-hour day and 180-day school year, that amounts to about seven years before you achieve expertise as a teacher. [32]

Teaching is indeed a reflective practice. Teaching is also a repetitive practice. Both of these give you opportunities for improvement. Veteran teachers have

---

[31] As an aside, I recommend making routine decisions as quickly as possible and moving forward. In the big picture, many decisions (for example, how much credit should I give this test response) are not very important and if you make a mistake you can correct it at a later time. You can save a lot of time that would otherwise be wasted fretting over minutiae.

[32] An eight-hour day is, of course, a conservative estimate. From my first time in the classroom, like most of us, I have spent many 10-12 hour school days, as well as much additional time on weekends. This would reduce that seven-year estimate. As I stated earlier, I didn't truly feel confident in my abilities as a teacher until my fifth year. That probably does meet Gladwell's 10,000-hour rule as my experience included teaching during grad school, and teaching summer courses.

learned to take advantage of the fact that the next class, the next day, the next semester, and the next year all provide opportunities for a 'doover'. They 'reflect' – what didn't go well, what they would like to change, and how they will try do better next time. Don't be afraid to take advantage of these opportunities to change your approach.

Find a trustworthy advisor or confidant

We all need the help of others to survive what appears at times to be a world against us. Hopefully you will find someone who can listen, offer advice, and ultimately understand what you are going through. Especially if you are having challenges with a particular student, or group of students, a colleague who shares those students can tell you if their experience with them is similar. Many times I've had teachers I work with put my mind at ease by relating that they too had difficulty with a particular student. This allowed me to shift my focus from my fear of having done something wrong to seeking a solution to the difficulties this student presented.

This doesn't have to be a school colleague. A family member or friend can provide a personal "shoulder to cry on." I don't mean that literally; rather, an outsider can serve as a sounding board, a listener who will give you a chance to tell your story and rethink it at the same time. That will give you a chance to place an episode in perspective and at the same time consider how best to address it this time or next.

Use your sense of humor

I am convinced that a sense of humor is at the top of the list of necessary teachers' characteristics. Being able to laugh at what your students have done and even more important at what you have done yourself can translate some of the worst events into not just an acceptable frame but into an entertainment.

Consider this through one of my own experiences. I was once a guide in Algonquin Park, a wild region of Canada about 200 miles north of Toronto. Among the many canoe trips I led, the one I remember most involved two days paddling and camping along the Crow River. I had looked forward to that trip, but it turned out to be quite different from what I expected. It rained every minute of the three days. We cooked over open wood fires that were very difficult to start and just as difficult to keep going. The water poured down so hard that a bowl of soup was cooled and diluted before we could taste our first spoonful. Our equipment and provisions were soaked, our campsites flooded. It was a terrible but thankfully brief time. The only good thing about the trip that I recall was taking out our canoes at the end. But that is the trip that I most remember and, whenever I meet friends who were with me then, we laugh over our experiences.

In exactly the same way on reflection the worst episodes that happen in your classroom can make the best stories. And those worst episodes can place the trivial episodes that happen daily in perspective. "This was nothing compared to what happened in my fifth period back in '16," can make you feel much better.

You'll also find that sharing your problems with your colleagues in a humorous frame will draw from them reminiscences that you will often find far worse and thus even more entertaining than your own.

PEOPLE

Letter Seventeen: Students

> *Bill and Mary in your classroom are far from abstractions,*
> *and the book rules often do not fit them.*
> *You can't hope to find in any school or book*
> *the intimate detailed knowledge you need*
> *about the 30 or 40 real, wriggling, squirming, fascinating,*
> *live, constantly changing units in your classroom.*
> --George Miller

When I was director of the Minnesota National Laboratory we gathered test results from thousands of high school math students in five mid-western states. In doing so each year we found high scoring students grouped in the classrooms of a few teachers whom we identified as outstanding. What surprised us, however, was that in the following year the same phenomenon occurred but the list of teachers was entirely different. Those we had identified the previous year were not among them.

What we were seeing was something that we had not expected but that we should have known: the particular group of students as well as their teacher contribute to a successful class.

You will find this true in your own teaching. You will enjoy working with the students in some classes but those in others will make you ready to climb your classroom walls.

Students are, of course, what your job is all about. Your role is to educate each of them in the very best way you can.

You will often hear it said that teachers should love their

students. This is simply nonsense. In fact, there is an aspect of this "requirement" that is off-putting. Surely love is an emotion that should be reserved for a different kind of relationship. You need not even like each student in your classes. Among them you will find all kinds of irritating adolescents: sneaks, liars, cheats, show-offs, bullies and even an occasional psychopath like my junior high school student who had been caught torturing cats and dogs.

At the opposite extreme you will almost certainly find students with attractive qualities: hard workers, high achievers and, yes, boys and girls you find physically or emotionally engaging. You would be inhuman if you did not find this to be the case. Of course, you will prefer these students and wish there were more like them.

Okay, you can like some, dislike others. What is required is that you must find a way to accommodate to each of them. And you must also avoid letting your preferences affect your academic support for and evaluation of your students.

I suggest that you think of your students in two very different ways: as members of a group in your classroom and as individuals outside that classroom.

Think about this in terms of your own experience as a high school student. Unless you were very independent, your views and your behavior were strongly influenced by your classmates. You laughed with them; you joined them in their likes and dislikes, in their loves and hates; you were careful to guard your status among them; you wanted their attention and avoided their disregard.

Then think about any experiences you had one-to-one with any of your teachers. If you talked with them in private settings, your relationship was very different. Then you didn't have to defend your reputation with your classmates in order to save face in that public environment and you saw your teacher as an individual with whom you felt freer to communicate. What had in another setting been a confrontation then became a conversation.

I had an unusual experience that drove this home to me. I was in my classroom after school one day when the teacher monitoring the detention study hall next door rushed in to ask a favor. "I have an emergency at home," she said. "Will you please keep an eye on my students?" Of course I agreed and she ran off down the hall.

When I walked down to look in on the students, I was confronted with them walking out. Evidently when they heard that their teacher had to leave, they decided that they could leave as well. As they came toward me, I stepped in front of the leading student. "Stop," I said. When he didn't stop I brought my hands up to stop him, but he was so close that they struck his chest and tipped him off balance onto the floor. I don't know which of us was more astonished at this. But saying nothing, he got up and, together with his classmates, marched back into the room.

I was so upset at my action — striking a student, no matter whether it was inadvertent, was unacceptable in that school, as it is in most schools — that I worried about being in serious trouble. If this student or his classmates reported me, I might well lose my job.

Later that same night on the way home from school I stopped to get gas at a local filling station. Who should come out to man the gas pump but the same student. After cordially greeting me he went on to say, "You sure set me straight in school." Of course, I took the opportunity to explain my action and to apologize for its unexpected consequences. "No problem," was his final response and I think we both came away from that odd incident feeling that we each had a new friend.

I have just watched the film, *Freedom Writers*, a fictionalized account of teaching in a crime-ridden urban area. Few of you will confront such difficult circumstances and the film has many failings, but it does make an important point about students that is common to all classrooms: You have very little insight into the problems your students confront outside your classroom. Many of those problems are well above your ability or training to respond. For example, it is not your role to address broken homes or the violence, illness and hunger that are part of some of your students' lives. You probably will never know what the specific problems of your students are, which is just as well as many are not solvable. This suggests that, whenever possible, you should, in their words, "give them a little space."

An aspect of this is brought home by one of the training films used by a major airline for its employees. It shows a man falling as he gets out of bed, cutting himself shaving, spilling cereal on his trousers, getting a traffic ticket hurrying to the airport, standing in endless lines to check in, and finally early in his flight getting into a confrontation with a flight attendant. The flight attendant has no idea what is the source of the passenger's upsetting behavior, but has to address it as best she or he can. Even your best students can have days like this.

There is one more important aspect of your work with students. A story by Greg Baugher speaks to this:

> There was, in one of my classes, a student who was struggling, despite putting forth a significant amount of effort. He was a quiet, thoughtful young man, one who was well liked and who in the past had always done well in that class. However, he told me he was having difficulty understanding the content I was teaching and finally he revealed to me that he felt I had given up on him. Since this must have been hard for a senior boy to admit, I realized that this must have come from deep in his heart.
>
> This experience had a lasting, significant impact on my attitude toward not only that individual student

but also other students and my teaching in general. I realized that I had reached a point with this student at which I really wasn't committed to his success. I had indeed unconsciously given up on him, and in this episode I saw the beginnings of what could have developed into an apathy that I now realize many teachers develop after a few years of teaching. I determined that I would not only never give up on any of my students, but that I would try never to communicate the feeling that I might have done so. Since that time, I have had many students whose grades indicated it was very improbable that they would ever pass my course; yet, I continue to try not only always to be hopeful and supportive, but also not to convey doubt in their ability to succeed.

If you show interest in your students as individuals, they will repay you by being interested in what you are teaching. Eileen Schoaff has this to say:

> As a beginning teacher I had a remedial student who was failing all his classes except mine, in which he earned a B. Several colleagues approached me to ask if this intimidating young man had somehow pressured me to give him that grade. That was not the case. At the beginning of the year I had asked my students to fill out index cards telling me about their interests and goals. This boy indicated that he wanted to be an auto mechanic. I made it a point to tell him that there were schools sponsored by Ford, Chevrolet, Honda and other auto manufacturers that trained auto mechanics, but that they required high school graduation as a prerequisite. And I included in problem sets exercises that pertained to his and other students' interests. This boy responded by earning that B grade.

Related to this are problems specific to math and often associated with the sciences as well. They are often subsumed under the term math anxiety. Many mathematics students, especially young women, are convinced that they are "no good at math" because they lack some inborn math trait. For 99% of students this is simply nonsense. Many of them will have picked up this excuse for not trying to learn in your classroom from comments made by their parents. For some of those parents, "I was never good in math," is an abbreviated form of "Look at what I achieved without being good at math." Never mind what more they could have achieved if they had worked at this subject.[33]

You will find this a difficult problem to address, but the more often you can create situations in which these students can succeed and you can point out to them how this contradicts their supposed genetic inferiority the better chance you will have of turning them around. Praise, well-earned and seriously given, is a powerful classroom tool.

One important study carried out recently showed that in science and mathematics classes boys were given much more time than girls to answer oral questions addressed to them by their teachers. When confronted with this evidence, the teachers — both male and female teachers — were shocked to realize that they had so discriminated against the girls.

---

[33] This problem was underscored in the early 1980s by a study by Julian Stanley and Camilla Benbow of Johns Hopkins University which purported to show that boys enjoy better native mathematics ability than girls. The basis for this claim was the better achievement of boys on challenging math tests.

My own experience with gifted students contradicts their claims. After the Johns Hopkins study gained national publicity, much attention was given to seeking ways to improve the achievement of young women. It became evident that young boys were more acculturated to mathematics than girls. Boys' toys were scientific — erector and chemistry sets — while girls' were social — dolls and playhouses. Boys were encouraged to achieve in the sciences, girls in social activities. When these differences were recognized and even partially addressed, the differences narrowed. Our experience in the University at Buffalo Gifted Math Program spoke to this. The proportion of girls who passed the challenging entrance examinations for this program went from 23% in 1980 to 50% in 1993. In that latter year the highest scoring young woman was a woman.

Sadly, the attention given to equalizing the achievement of young men and women in math and science has declined and today the proportion of girls in those Gifted Math Program classes has returned to about 35%. I urge you to think of ways in all classes to address this inequality.

Although I know of no similar study relating to minority students, I suspect that this same thing is true in their case as well.

This is something to which you should be sensitive. Time is always a factor in your teaching so there is always pressure to "move on," but that pressure should be the same in your dealings with all students.

Who Will Remember You?

A final point to consider: You will probably most enjoy teaching honor students, but they are not the ones who will remember you. They will go on to higher education and find stronger faculty associations there. The students you will see more often once they graduate are those in your remedial classes. Many more of them will remain in the school's local community. The message is clear. Of course you should seek to advance the knowledge of these weaker students, but there is a pay-off as well. When you inform these students and help them to gain appreciation for the beauty and utility of mathematics, you may well have contributed more to them than you gave to some of your more able students.

Letter Eighteen: Students Differences

> Try to recall how you felt at their age.
> —George Miller

Unless you are very fortunate — perhaps teaching in a private school where class sizes are often small — you will deal with students in groups of twenty to thirty.[33] Whatever the number of students in your classes, however, you will most often think of them as a group. You will plan your lessons for a full class; you will assign classroom exercises, homework assignments and quizzes in common. This is a matter of simple efficiency, but it is even more: there is a real sense that you owe your students equal treatment.

Providing equal treatment of your students is one of the best ways you can demonstrate acceptance of them all. Consistency in the way you stick to your classroom rules and procedures — and in particular disciplining your best students in the same way you do your worst — shows everyone that you hold them accountable.[34]

---

[33] There are exceptions: I recall complaining to a New York City parochial school teacher about the teaching loads - the number of classes and the total number of students in those classes - of my teachers in Norwalk, Connecticut. I told him, "Typical of our loads is a junior high teacher I visited today: he has 135 students in five classes." The priest's response: "I'm teaching 260 geometry students in six classes." All I could think was: geometry, of all subjects!

[34] One aspect of this relates to rewards for achievement and should probably be responded to individually. For some able students a 93 grade is as unacceptable as

Nevertheless, you should not forget your students' individual needs. They may do many things to look alike and act alike in order to belong, to fit in, to avoid being different from each other (while at the same time working hard to be very different from you and other adults) but they are not all cut from the same mold. They may run in packs, but those packs are made up of unique young men and women.

In this letter I alert you to a few of the categories into which individual students fit. I will also suggest some special concerns these categories raise, but the important point is that you should look for students like these and seek ways of addressing their special needs. These certainly do not exhaust the types of individual students, but they are ones that I have found turn up often.

Please understand: I don't have answers to these situations. I can only offer a few of the ways I and others have handled them successfully. (I will, of course, omit my many serious missteps in addressing these special boys and girls.)

Students in over their head

You are a bright person or you would never have been able to qualify as a teacher, so you may not be as sensitive to this kind of student as you should be. You may simply think of them as lazy or quitters. There are, of course, lazy students and quitters, but these students are different from them.[35]

---

a 73 grade is to a weak student. In this case it is achievement up to their ability which deserves equal treatment.

[35] I am especially sensitive to these students because, as I described earlier, I was one for a full year. It was in that English graduate program in which I found myself completely outclassed. In addition to that classmate who would later win the Pulitzer Prize for poetry and the one who later wrote

Often students are misdirected through forces not of their own design. Counselors or parents overrate them or, as I did, they overrate themselves. When you identify such students, you should discuss what you consider their inappropriate placement with your school guidance staff. But usually you'll still find yourself stuck with them just as they are stuck with you.

I urge you to go beyond helping these students with their work. Talk with them individually about the nature of their difficulties and the possible sources of their problems. Try too to have them identify areas outside your class in which they are successful. But most important, do two things: communicate to them that you are on their side and let them know that you honor them despite their problems.

Non-participants

This student is often characterized by his or her asking, "What do we need this for?" Don't fall into the trap of listing a series of reasons why your subject is important. Very few students really care about the utility of their courses: school is just something they put up with. You'll rarely hear that question from a successful student. It is simply a generalized complaint and one response is simply to ask, "Where are you having difficulty?"

Alternatively, you can do as Ray Patenaude did. His response to this inquiry is: "Never mind when or if you'll ever use this. The State of South Carolina has paid me to teach this

---

Broadway plays; others contributed to major journals, one wrote novels. For me the phrase, "in over your head", was dead on: each day in our classes I felt as though I was drowning. Fortunately, I escaped with only wounded pride. But that terrible experience did make that positive contribution to my teaching. I find myself better able to relate to students trapped like I had been in a setting they can in no way manage successfully.

to you, and it is something you'll have to do now in order to reach whatever goals you and I have." After saying this a few times at the beginning of the year he finds himself no longer challenged by this question and students see that he isn't dissuaded from the job he has been hired to do.

Like all of us, our students have priorities and for almost all of them math is well down on their list. If you can somehow associate your subject with those priorities for this withdrawn student, you will help both the student and yourself.

Of course, each student is different but consider how I reached out to one: "Walter, you're a fine athlete and you've got plenty of brains to be successful in this class as well. Your athletic ability will certainly help you obtain college scholarship support but you'll also need to pass examinations to meet their minimum standards. I can help you meet those requirements if you'll let me." That student came back to thank me after he gained admission to Seton Hall University. Walter Dukes later played for the Globetrotters and in the NBA.

Sadly, there may be a health-associated reason for a student's non-participation. We do have poor students suffering from malnutrition in our schools and you need to watch for these cases. You may not be able to help them yourself, but you can at least communicate such specific problems to your counseling staff.

Gifted students

Be thankful when you find bright, creative students in your classroom. These students will inevitably make you look good — just as the students who cannot master the content you teach will make you look bad no matter how hard you work with them. There is a real sense, however, that you can accept what talented students bring to your class without offering those students anything in return.

And this is simply wrong.

We are training gifted students to be lazy in our schools. Given their talents, they can drift along, achieving excellent grades without the kind of effort demanded of their classmates. You need to think seriously about how to address this problem.

For years one national program designed for gifted math students simply piled on mindlessly designed work. While their classmates answered the odd numbered exercises in a standard text, they had these students answer all the exercises.

Why the students accepted this nonsense was beyond me.

They had been bamboozled into thinking that their participation in a program sponsored by a major university was right for them.

Instead you need to find more appropriate avenues into which to channel their energies. You might provide them with a different text and suggest that they compare the approaches to class activities in that text and the one used by their classmates. This can be in place of their doing some of the mundane exercises assigned to their classmates.

You should also encourage these students to look beyond their local school for programs that will stimulate them. Some of our finest authors got their start writing for children's magazines like Kazoo and Boy's Life and National Geographic Kids. There are all kinds of essay-writing contests, from those sponsored by NASA to those sponsored by the United Institute of Peace. There are math competitions to encourage your students to enter and dozens of science activities, everything from local science fairs to national robotic tournaments.

You and your gifted students will be overwhelmed when you begin to search out these programs, many of which offer fiscal support for students in need. You'll need to provide some supportive guidance here.

In providing that guidance you need to know your own

limits. You need to beware of limiting these bright kids to programs with which you are familiar or even associated. And new programs seem to pop up every day.

One experience of mine reminds me of my own limitations. Because I studied at the University of Rochester whose Eastman School of Music is recognized as a competitor of the nearly incomparable Julliard School in New York City, I was approached by a music student when I was teaching in Johnson City, New York. He asked me about the Eastman programs. I told him about one program with which I was familiar that I thought he should enter in order "to get his feet wet," that is to see how deep was his interest and ability. I soon learned that this student was a far better musician than I had assumed and that the appropriate program for him was well advanced from the one I had recommended.

You may enjoy working with bright students individually but often you will find the best of them too much of a personal challenge as was that music student. Some teachers have contacted college faculty or workers in related fields in industry to work with such students independently.

Two basic rules apply here: (1) These students represent a national resource, and (2) They need just as much personal attention as your weaker students.

Irrepressible students

Loudmouth. Show off. Spoiled brat.[36] Selfish jerk (or often a far more serious un-publishable expletive). These are some of the ways you will hear this student described in the teacher's lounge. Some of these students may be

---

[36] A related neologism as it applies here is affluenza for being spoiled by wealthy parents. It is a portmanteau word combining affluence with influenza.

ADHD[37] and those should be referred to your guidance department for appropriate treatment. More often, they are simply irrepressible adolescents.

Never mind a diagnosis of their problems, are you going to let such students take over your classrooms, ruin your lessons and prevent their classmates from learning? Surely not.

Here is a case that is quite different from the others I have introduced, because you *have to* address this problem and you must address it immediately as it will only get worse. If you confront these students in class, however; you will simply play into their game. They seek attention and you will be contributing to the scenario they seek to accomplish.[38]

My response to several of these students has followed the pattern of this example. I had been warned about a boy before he joined my class and the first time he interrupted my lesson, I walked over to his desk, leaned over and whispered, "Show me the schedule of your classes." He was clearly unprepared for my approach but, because I was whispering, he did so as well. "Here it is," he responded, opening his notebook. I continued, "I see you have 5th period free. I have that period free as well. I can't have you in this class interrupting me, so I am going to take you next door to study hall now and I will have to teach you during that period." He clearly wasn't happy about this — needless to say, I wasn't either — but I gave him no alternative. I marched him to the study hall and with the proctor's assistance found him a seat.

When he showed up during my free period I told him that this was an extreme imposition on my time, but that I was

---

[37] ADHD is Attention Deficit Hyperactivity Disorder, a diagnosis recognized by the World Health Organization's International Classification of Diseases.
[38] I have also found that students are most "vulnerable" early in the school year. They are facing many new things – new friends, new courses, new teachers – and at this time they respond well to special attention. Later in the year they will have become more comfortable in their behavior and difficult to change.

prepared to teach him separately from his classmates so long as he was unwilling to behave in my class. I then went over the work we had covered that morning. Like many of these disruptive students, he was intelligent and picked up the concepts quickly and easily.

After two days of this, the student asked if he could return to his regular class. I approved but with the condition that any misbehavior on his part would lead us back to this program. In fact it did for just one more day later in the year, but we got along quite well the rest of the time.

There is even a sequel to this story. I taught this same student again two years later. He had by then gained control of his behavior and was a classroom contributor rather than a detractor.

Students confronting each other

As if you don't have enough problems, now you have to teach students who hate each other. My experience has been that this has more often been a problem between young women than between young men, but it arises for both.

Talking to the two students together outside class may help, but you have to work through the "you said" "no, you said" circular claims before you have any chance of making headway. The best you may be able to do is tell the students that they don't have to like each other, but that they dishonor themselves by such behavior. And, most important, you will not tolerate their forming cliques in your classroom.

I first tried addressing this situation in my classes by seating such students far apart, but then I decided to force them to confront their attitudes by not only seating them next to each other but forcing them to work together on tasks. I then went out of my way to congratulate them on working through their problems and I added that the world is not full of best friends. In at least a few cases this worked out very well.

Students infatuated with you[39]

At first having your students regard you favorably may massage your ego. I know it did mine when, still an undergraduate, I substituted for a month in an urban school where I was thirty years younger than the next oldest teacher. For several days young women jammed the door of my classroom between periods to see what a young teacher looked like. But that was quite different from individual students being infatuated with you. This can be a very challenging situation.

You may have heard the story of the teacher who was sent a love letter by a student. The teacher penciled grammatical errors in the letter and returned it for corrections.[40] Although that has occasionally been cited as a humorous response, I find it offensive. Yes, it sent the message that a teacher lives in a different world, but it also told the young woman that her (in this case) feelings weren't worth considering.

Of course, the first two rules are: Do not encourage such infatuation and, even more important, never return it and get involved with a student. If you break the second rule, you are no longer a teacher; you are a felon who should be rejected from the teaching profession.

Those rules are obvious, but they say nothing about how to handle the genuine affection that individual students feel for

---

[39] This section applies equally to male teachers teaching female students and female teachers teaching male students.
[40] This led to tragic consequences in the book and film *Up the Down Staircase*.

you. You need to be sympathetic but you also need to communicate to the student that you do not, cannot and will not return their affection overtly even though you appreciate it.

And you may need to get help with this. I had an episode during my second year of teaching that eventually led me to discuss the "forward" conversations of one young woman with my administrator. We brought the student and her mother to the office to discuss the situation and, fortunately, it was resolved in ways that were eventually satisfying to all of us.

Special Education students[41]

Years ago students with disabilities were segregated from their peers in separate classrooms. Today instead, most of them are main-streamed in regular classrooms. They usually come, however, with specific educational plans with which you must familiarize yourself. You should also discuss these students with special education staff; they will have suggestions about ways to assist these young men and women who are indeed special.

The most important point about these students is that, unless there is some specific restriction in their plan, your expectations for them should be exactly the same as your expectations for the other students in your classes. Special ed staff may suggest additional ways of helping these students, but they should be in addition to and not replacements for your regular classroom activities.

In fact, it has been my experience that what works for these students, works for everybody. When you add activities that serve such individuals — such things as

---

[41] My daughter, Susan Kelch, administrator of an urban special education program, provided information for this section.

memory devices and multi-sensory approaches — you serve all of your students better.

Young Women

Whether you are a male or female teacher you should recognize the differences between young men and young women that affect their learning. Of course there are exceptions, but generally boys are more forward and aggressive than girls. If nothing else, they are simply larger.

And boys can easily dominate your attention.

Keep in mind the finding, mentioned earlier, of that carefully controlled research study that the questioning of boys was very different from the questioning of girls. Young men were found to receive much more time to answer questions while teachers quickly turned to another student when young women didn't respond immediately. What was especially interesting about that study was the fact that the teachers involved all thought that they were giving equal treatment to both sexes.

Our society contributes to problems that young women have with math and science. As I pointed out, we raise our girls differently from our boys. Girls are encouraged to play with homemaking equipment while boys play with toys more related to science and math. Then we are surprised when young women excel in reading while boys outdo them in math and science.[42]

What should you do about this? At least be alert to gender differences in your classrooms. Try hard to equalize your acceptance of the achievements of your students so that girls

---

[42] For more on this including additional references see:
https://courses.lumenlearning.com/educationalpsychology/chapter/genderdifferences-in-the-classroom/

are not bypassed. And encourage young women individually whenever you can.

Although I have left this concern until last in this chapter, that does not indicate its importance. In fact, I consider this one of the most important concerns we face in all education. Young women represent a significant national scientific resource that is being seriously undervalued.

Letter Nineteen: Colleagues

> *Beware of drifting into that large group of teachers who think that teaching school would be an attractive occupation were it not for the pupils.*
> —George Miller

Like zebras, your teaching colleagues will come in stripes of many patterns. You'll find them as different in ability, in personality and in appearance as your students. Some will serve as wonderful models of teaching quality, as did several of my own; but a few will make you wonder why anyone hired them and how they achieved tenure. Sadly, it tends to be those latter teachers who will characterize your school in the eyes of the public.

I share with you two things I found about my colleagues over the years, almost all of whom I genuinely liked and respected.

First, in general teachers are very conservative. I am not talking here about politics: in fact their politics is more often progressive. Rather, I am talking about their attitude toward teaching, their students and even their subject. The descriptive phrase is: set in their ways. And why not? What they have done they feel works for them and their students. Why change?

You should be prepared for this. If you propose to do something different, don't expect ready acceptance by your peers.

The second aspect of their behavior is that they will be far better prepared to criticize than to commend. They share this quality with the rest of us. As one of my college English professors told us, "The critical faculty is easy to foster; commendations are far less readily drawn." I urge you to be aware of this and to fight against it in your own behavior. As Greg Baugher has put it very well:

There is nothing to be gained by blaming anyone in teaching and learning. We should not blame the student, unless there is direct non-cooperation or misbehavior. We should not blame the teacher as long as he or she is sincerely trying to reach the students and help them learn. And we should not blame parents, administrators, or anyone else in the situation. Such acts of personal, directed blame for others is just a waste of energy and is not profitable.

In this regard consider my experience teaching students in a wealthy suburban school district. The boys especially were often silly and disruptive and they went out of their way to play tricks on teachers. One semester they invented a student and somehow had him assigned to a full regimen of classes. After the student's "parents" had produced a month of absence excuses, they went one step further: they reported the student to the local police as a drug supplier. It took the school administration some effort to understand what was going on and then to untangle the mess. At Halloween, these same students managed somehow to raise an art teacher's Volkswagen onto the roof of the school bus barn.

Here was truly creative behavior.

Many of my colleagues did not accept this silliness for what it was. Instead, they hated these students and I am convinced that in some cases this hatred even carried over into the grades they assigned. I was shocked by the way these students were described in the teacher's lounge. A few, for disciplinary reasons, were even placed in remedial programs. Yet these were the same students who were performing well in my advanced classes. Yes, they were always ready to be

disruptive but, as soon as they saw that I disassociated their behavior from their academic achievement, I had them on my side. But still some of my colleagues could not accept how and why I got along with them.

I do not wish to send the wrong message by this example. I certainly do not encourage you to take your students' side against other teachers. This is a trap into which many beginners fall and you can rightly be charged with inappropriate behavior. Rather, I have offered it to encourage you to make your own judgments about your students and not simply to take what others offer.

Blaming Your Predecessors

One of the easiest traps into which you can easily fall is blaming those who taught your students last year or even earlier for all their deficiencies.[43] The blogger educationrealist[44] speaks to this cogently when he describes what happens when you reteach "what those earlier instructors failed to teach."

At first, it seems to work. The kids beam and say, "You explain it so much better than my last teacher did!" and the quizzes seem to show real progress. Phew! Now it's possible to get on to teaching algebra, rather than the material the kids just hadn't been taught.

---

[43] I liken this to my daughter who, as she progressed through elementary school always deferred to her current teacher but referred to her earlier instructors as "those baby teachers."

[44] See http://educationrealist.wordpress.com/.

But then, a few weeks later, the kids go back to ignoring the difference between 3 – 5 and 5 – 3. Furthermore, despite hours of explanation and practice, half the class seems to do no better than toss a coin to make the call on positive or negative slopes. Many students who demonstrated mastery of distributing multiplication over addition are now making a complete hash of the process in multi-step equations.

And many students are still counting on their fingers. It's as if they weren't taught at all.

You should not only remember this near universal effect but also realize that next year's failures will be blamed on you.

The Experiences of Five Beginners

Janet Shiver[45] interviewed five first year elementary school teachers about their experiences trying to work with their fellow teachers. These insightful newcomers identified four types of colleagues: concerned peers, jealous peers, negative peers and uninterested peers. Sadly the beginners found none of these types helpful to them. Concerned colleagues in trying to assist them simply sought to impose on them their own accepted behavior. Jealous colleagues resented any success they achieved. Negative colleagues rejected change and new ideas. And uninterested colleagues wanted no part of any cooperative activity.

Secondary school teachers are rarely asked to work as closely with their colleagues as were these beginners and in no school did I ever identify as many such crass colleagues as they did. It also may be that the interview format led these beginners to exaggerate their interactions with their colleagues. But even if that is the

---

[45] In her doctoral thesis. See the Literature Cited for the source of this interesting document.

case, the experiences of these elementary school teachers describe some of the negative characteristics you may find in some of your school colleagues.

On a Less Somber Note

I cannot resist adding here two stories about fellow teachers. At the end of my first school year, the male teachers went out to lunch together. During the meal they announced to me that this was an annual event and that the youngest teacher was always expected to pay the bill. And moreover, I was the youngest. You can just imagine how that made me feel: I was quite literally frightened. Did I even have enough money to cover the cost? But when the quite substantial bill arrived and was handed to me, the teachers began to pass me money to cover their meals. When I sorted it all out, I found enough not only to pay the bill and cover a substantial tip but also to pay for my own food.

That worked out so well that, when I moved to another school and joined my fellow teachers at a similar luncheon, I suggested that we do the same thing. Mistake! These teachers were not nearly so generous and I found myself having to give $20 to my younger colleague who got the bill so that he wouldn't be so deeply shortchanged.

I don't think that those experiences indicate something wrong with the teachers in the second school. Rather, it suggests that you need to pick and choose situations in which you can trust your colleagues.

Now consider how a teacher evaluation was conducted in the school of a Pennsylvania friend. His district announced a merit pay program and all teachers were to be evaluated, the best to receive extra salary increments. And in this rural district the superintendent would carry out the evaluation single-handed. He would visit the classrooms of every teacher in every school in his district. As the evaluations began to pile up, it became clear that the superintendent had a hearing problem. Each teacher was recorded as not speaking loudly enough.

In my friend's school was one of those coaches who doubled as a middle school science teacher. Clearly unqualified and unprepared for that role, he showed movies to his classes on most days. But when the superintendent showed up to evaluate him, the coach showed extraordinary creativity. "Today," he announced to his class, "we're going to study artificial respiration." "And sir," he went on, turning to the superintendent, "would you please come up front to serve as our victim?" Needless to say, that coach was the only teacher in that school building to receive a merit increment.

Although that episode was unique, it speaks to just one of the problems with merit pay. If you are reasonably successful as a young teacher, you may find the concept of such rewards attractive and indeed theoretically merit pay has its merits. It is in the implementation that it fails. On what is the evaluation based? Who does the evaluating?

Consider one proposal that a committee in a school in which I was teaching came up with in response to a state merit initiative. The proposed evaluation included 30% for community activities and 25% for care of the room in which you taught. After other factors were included only 11% was left for presentation of content. When we were presented with this proposal, several of us were outraged. What bothered me the most was that proposal that community activities count at all. We were hired as teachers and, although most of us did contribute as scout leaders and Chamber of Commerce members, that was not part of our job.

Fortunately that entire state initiative came to naught.

Support Personnel

I cannot end this letter without mentioning two very important school staff roles: school secretaries and school custodians. As Murray Siegel points out, next to the principal these are the most important people in your school. Remove them and school operation would grind to a halt. Their jobs are very different from yours but they merit your respect. You should make every effort to get on their good side.

In fact, they know students from their very different perspectives and can often provide you with insights you and your teaching colleagues cannot gain in your classroom interactions with those students. Value their independence and take advantage of it by discussing with them in informal settings their observations of your charges. They might know, for example, that a particular student is faced with a difficult situation outside the school.

*

Your best bet: as a beginner you will be expected to act like a beginner. Pitch in, do your job, cooperate with others, be pleasant, never criticize and in particular try not to make waves. As one of my best but quietest students once told me, "I just keep a low profile." That approach can serve you well in your first months in school.

Letter Twenty: Administrators

> *The principal is always right,*
> *misinformed perhaps,*
> *maybe a little sloppy, sometimes a bit crude,*
> *fickle, bullheaded, even stupid,*
> *but never wrong!*
> —principal's desk sign

    A few years ago I spent a semester teaching in England, where in many junior schools there is no one identified as principal. Each school has an individual temporarily elected as head teacher. This person teaches a regular schedule but also carries administrative responsibilities for the school. We have nothing like that here. Our principals have usually but not always had teaching experience, but their role now is very different. They are no longer identified with us classroom teachers.[46] In fact some of them see themselves in an adversarial role opposed to the members of their staffs.

    Keep in mind that school administrators have many non-instructional responsibilities. They must work with nonteaching personnel, handle matters related to the school buildings and grounds, address student transportation problems, and work with a school budget. They must also deal with their own bosses, usually district superintendents, and with the general public and the school board. We should

---

[46] I note one exception to this separation. One of my finest principals, Myron White, had been a math teacher and had even written math texts. He taught a remedial math class and we arranged my schedule so that I could substitute for him when he had to be away to attend district meetings.

appreciate the fact that their workday is beset with mundane non-academic activities.

Unfortunately, however, this means that hiring, mentoring and firing teachers, and administering the instructional program often find their place far down the list of issues to be addressed by them.

You should keep in mind your administrators' many responsibilities in working with them. Realize that what you want from a principal or supervisor must battle with these other items on their immediate priority list.

An Informal Poll

Before writing this letter I did some homework. I listed all the principals and school superintendents with whom I was associated either as a student, teacher, department head or supervisor. My list included thirty-six principals and six superintendents. I then evaluated — subjectively, of course — those school leaders on their contribution to the academic program of their schools. Of the principals I rated only half good or excellent. The superintendents fared better overall: five good, one bad, but the latter was so bad that I consider him evil.[47]

Now remember: I was rating those school leaders on just one facet of their responsibility. And of course I saw them through the lens of a person with concern only for classroom instruction. Having said that, however, I believe that my assessment suggests that many schools are shortchanged in their academic leadership.

I was fortunate to have worked with the high quality

---

[47] I hate even to recall this superintendent but I offer one of his minor tricks as evidence of his character. When he and his assistant met with a individual staff member, he would tape the session, giving it the quality of a police interrogation.

administrators on my list. I respected them for their leadership and their service to their students and staffs. They showed the qualities you associate with good leaders of any kind: seriousness of purpose, focus on task, evenhandedness, respect for quality and loyalty to those who serve with them.

As educators they were also serious about their concern for communicating subject content and process.

I offer here a story about his loyalty to staff of one of those principals. In addition to my duties as a first year teacher in his high school, I supervised a community play center evenings. There I had a confrontation with an eighth grade boy. When time came to close the facility, this boy paid no attention to my request that the basketballs be returned and went on playing. To get his attention I tossed a volleyball at him. The ball went the length of the court and, much to my surprise, hit the boy in the rump. Of course this didn't injure him but it shocked and embarrassed him in front of his peers. He swore, yelled, "I'll fix you," and stormed out of the play center, slamming the door so hard it was a wonder it didn't break.

The next morning as I was picking up my mail at the high school, my principal motioned me into his office. "There's a call for you," he said and handed me the phone. When I identified myself, I found myself being scolded by the boy's enraged mother. Explaining what happened did nothing to quell the woman's anger.

After a minute or two listening to this my principal said, "Let me have that telephone," and he grabbed it from me, identified himself to the mother and asked for her son's name. He then went on to tell her that I was one of his school's finest teachers, that he didn't want me upset by coddling parents because he didn't want to lose me, that he had noted her son's name and would watch for further problems when in another year the boy would enter the high school. He finished with a recommend-dation that the mother discipline her child and, without giving her a chance to respond, cradled the phone. Turning to me he said simply, "That should take care of that.

Now forget that episode."

I could hardly believe what I had heard and, laughing, blurted out my thanks. Needless to say, I have considered that principal one of the heroes of my early teaching career.

Don't get me wrong. There are times when we in education pull up the drawbridge and refuse to respond to quite reasonable concerns of outsiders. This, I believe, was not one of those times.

In fact, I join Art DiVito in believing that "no teachers should ever be made to feel, in their life's career, that they have to tip-toe about broken glass to perform their job." And I wonder if today the ending of that story might be very different.

While I deeply appreciated such supportive principals, I question how some of the poorer administrators I worked with were selected and even retained in their roles. To me they represent one of our schools' greatest problems: a failure of leadership. Almost all of the teachers in those poorly administered schools felt let down by the person assigned as their leader. Perhaps my rating of them is too harsh, but my estimate suggests that you will have a good chance of working under an administrator who will be less than helpful.

When I was a city supervisor, I recall working with a principal in one school about specific problems she had identified for each of her teachers. We discussed in some detail how we would help them address their problems. But then I drove a quarter mile to another school where the principal knew nothing about what was going on in his classrooms. All he could tell me was, "Any help you can give these teachers will be well received."

It is clear to me that the Peter Principle too often applies in our schools.

Supervisory Visits

Good administrators, including department heads and supervisors if your school has them, can be especially supportive of beginning teachers. You may not recognize things you do that cause problems for you and your students. Their mentoring suggestions can serve you even if you consider and reject some of their ideas, because they force you to think about those identified aspects of your instruction.

In fact any administrators who visit your classroom, whether they be good or bad, will provide you with an odd kind of bonus. Your students see these outsiders as authority figures "picking on" you and they take your side. For these brief moments you and your students will be working together.

What does all this mean to you? You almost certainly had no choice about the administrator of the school in which you teach. You must then work with him or her and, in the case of a weak administrator, you may also need to work around your boss. You know from your own experience as a student what that is like. At that time and for your own sake you worked for all of your teachers but sometimes around the poor ones.

I do not mean this letter to make you paranoid about the leaders of your school. Instead, I urge you to be aware of your administrators' and supervisors' roles and simply to find a way to work for them in the best way possible. At the same time I suggest that you should be sensitive to possible problems. Be aware of the distinction between you and your administrators, just as I have urged you to be aware of the distinction between you and your students.

Letter Twenty-one: Parents

> *Fight against the feeling that you are a mere transient,*
> *and develop the conviction that,*
> *contrary to the expectations of others,*
> *you are as much a regular citizen*
> *as anyone in town.*
> —George Miller

Two stories

One: At a high school I had just joined, in our initial meeting with the school guidance counselors we new teachers were instructed, "Do not communicate with your students' parents."

That edict seemed wrong-headed to me: surely we want to have those adults on our side. They can oversee their children's homework and can side with us in encouraging achievement. After the meeting I shared with the counselor this view and asked him why we shouldn't work with parents. His response: "If you complain to a parent about the work of their child in this city, you may be endangering that child's life. This rule was instituted after we had several students seriously injured after such contacts."

Of course, that episode took place many years ago in a town largely populated by recent immigrants to this country, immigrants who were very serious strivers. They saw education as all-important to their children and in their effort to support us some of them punished their kids in the only way they knew: they beat them severely.

Two: Compare that story with another of my favorites. Bob Davies, the discipline officer (his more exalted title was vice principal) of my suburban school told me about one of my junior high school students. This student's class was staging an operetta and the boy collected stones and threw them at the performers from the auditorium balcony. Learning of this, Bob raced up to the balcony only to see the student depart through another door. He chased the student out of the school building and across the school lawn, failing to catch him but picking up a pint bottle, half full of liquor, that the student dropped.

The following Monday at Bob's request the student's mother appeared in his office to learn about her son's latest offence. Bob told her the story and at the end he drew the bottle from his drawer and informed the mother that the boy had dropped it. The mother's prompt response, "Why don't we have a little nip?"

Those to me represent two extremes of teacher-parent contact. Clearly there should be a better middle ground. While not all parents are able to help their children with the content you are teaching, especially when your school is implementing a new curriculum, most will at least attempt to work with you to improve their child's achievement. And, if you work out ways to help them do so, they can at least keep track of their youngster's homework record.

It is my strong belief that you should seek by every means possible to get your students' parents on your side. And I am also convinced that the best way to do this is to communicate with them in positive settings before problems arise. If you wait until you have uncomfortable confrontations with students, working with their parents at that time will be far more difficult. Most parents in seeking the best for their children will take those youngsters' side if they are in trouble.

Surely you would do the same.

One of the settings in which you may meet parents is at a Parent-Teacher Conference, often on a school night set aside for such activities. Of course those sessions are generally attended by the parents of your best students, which is a perfect indication of the role of supportive parents. You will, however, sometimes find yourself confronting the parents of one of your worst students. This can be discountenancing but your responsibility is to make clear to the parents that their youngster's behavior or accomplishments fall short of your expectations. If you can see beyond your students' behavior and genuinely like them, you can place these concerns in a positive fashion, something like, "I'm really pleased to meet Mary's parents. I'm sure that she has told you about some of our confrontations, and indeed we have had far too many. But I really like Mary: she has spunk and I appreciate that. I only wish she didn't consider me her opponent. I want to help her and I'm having difficulty doing so. Can you and I find a way to reach out to her?" Parents are often defensive about their children even if they too are having difficulties with them. If you start out in this fashion, you will often find that you share problems with their child and you'll at least find yourselves on the same side.

In what was to me the most frightening episode of my early career in teaching, I was involved in a confrontation with a student when I was refereeing a basketball game in the school gymnasium. A player became so upset at a foul call that he attacked me, fists swinging. As he grappled with me, I raised my arm to signal a technical foul and my elbow brushed the player's cheek. His coach stormed out onto the court yelling at me for hitting his player. Fortunately the other official came to my defense with the coach and we were able to control the episode and the game before the fans came out of the stands, something that happens too often in small towns.[48]

As reports of such episodes often will, the story soon expanded and spread rapidly. Soon it came back to me that I had "severely beaten" a high school student. I was deeply upset about the incident and, sure enough, the call came from my principal's office the next morning that I was to report there immediately.

I arrived to find the boy and his father together with my principal and I felt that I was entering the lion's den. The father was a 300-pound giant, a furious giant at that. My principal, who knew nothing about this incident, asked the father what his visit was all about and the father repeated the now widespread story. He said simply, "I've learned that this guy beat up my kid." As he said this, he appeared ready to lunge at me.

Knowing that I had somehow to get this mess back into line, I turned to the student. "Harvey," I said, "will you please tell me what you have told your father." The boy, looking down at his shoes, blubbered something like, "You hit me."

I turned back to the father and said, "I can understand your concern about someone hitting your son without provocation, but please let me tell my side of this story. Harvey, you correct me if and when you disagree with what I say." And I went through the complete story of the episode, finishing by saying, "I'm really sorry that my elbow hit you, Harvey, but I was only trying to respond to your behavior." During this recitation Harvey continued to look at his shoes. When I finished, I turned to him and asked if my story was inaccurate. "I was just hitting you on the arms," was all he mumbled.

---

[48] At another basketball game my refereeing partner was hit over the head with a heavy pocketbook carried by a player's mother. Still another in our section had his jaw broken by an incensed player. Basketball officiating is too often a contact sport.

The father's response to this was as unexpected as it was electric. He ordered his son, "Get out to the car and I will have more to say to you there." And he turned to me: "I'm embarrassed about this incident, and I apologize for it," he said and he offered me his hand. I was very happy to take it.

*

Many educated parents have strong views about various aspects of school instruction. Those views may differ markedly from your own. While you should respect their views, I have found that making clear your own positions and courteously countering their arguments will do you no harm. You should make it very clear, however, that such discussions are separate from your efforts together to assist their children.

GOING FURTHER

Letter Twenty-two: A Bag of Tricks[49]

> *I like the teacher who gives you something to take home to think about besides homework.*
> —Lily Tomlin

Paul Rosenbloom enjoyed an international reputation as a senior mathematician when I joined his Minnemath Project at the University of Minnesota as his assistant director. His *Elements of Mathematical Logic* remains today a basic resource recognized worldwide to be of historical as well as academic significance.

In our very first conversation he told me that he considered teaching outside the classroom an important aspect of a mathematician's life and he urged me to develop what he called "a bag of tricks" from which to draw math-related lessons for people of all ages. I would later see him draw from his own collection in a number of settings. He could captivate anyone from nursery school students to scientific colleagues and even senior political figures.

Within a month of that conversation I found myself seated on an airplane flying from Minneapolis to Denver. My seat partners were a bored ten-year-old and her mother. When the mother learned that I was a math teacher, she asked me if I would be willing to "show Marjorie some math."

Fortunately, I had been reading David Silverman's book,

---

[49] Winnie Peterson suggested an alternate title for this letter, *Share, Save and Steal*, a phrase first suggested by Max Sobel about collecting such activities.

Your Move, and I had some pennies with me. I played a series of Nim games with Marjorie, finding her an interested opponent and a remarkably quick study.[50]

Our time together went very fast as Marjorie quickly mastered the various games I showed her. Before I knew it, we were well on our descent into the Denver airport. I was rewarded for our hour together when Marjorie turned to her mother to tell her that she wanted to become a mathematician.

Because the story has an unexpected positive conclusion, I will tell you about my use of a lesson copied from the remarkable teacher, Robert Wirtz.[52]

Late one school year when I was a math supervisor I was asked by a primary school teacher to demonstrate Stern blocks for her students. Stern blocks are inch cross-section blocks that come in lengths from one to ten inches. Cuisenaire rods are similar but with centimeter dimensions.

I took several sets of Stern blocks to this teacher's classroom and showed the six-year-olds some of the relationships among them. The children were excited by the opportunity to mix play with learning, and I was convinced that they were gaining from the lesson. I noticed, however, that their teacher was not happy with the children's mix of play with learning. Several times she interrupted their activities to tell individuals to be quiet.

It was clear to me that the teacher was convinced that I wasn't disciplining the children in the way she

---

[50] Nim, for readers unfamiliar with the word, is German for "take" and in this context it applies to games with players taking one or more counters like coins from a collection following a given set of rules. There are many nim games. [52] Bob Wirtz and his wife adopted a number of children with severe learning problems and they developed math materials to teach them. With Mark Botel, then president of the International Reading Association, he gathered those materials into books for elementary school students. I knew both of these men and especially honored their unusual association. Sadly, their textual materials are difficult to find today for they include some very attractive activities.

wished, so I suggested that I would like to return the next day to teach another lesson. Despite her apparent reservations about my conduct of this class, she jumped at the chance to have another class taught by an outsider. It was clear that she was happy to pass responsibility for these irrepressible kids off onto anyone she could find.

I had seen Wirtz teach a lesson to a similar group and the next day I followed his model. Before we started I had the teacher gather the students to sit on the floor in front of a chalkboard. Saying nothing to them I drew a square on the board and within it marked two star shapes. What I had drawn looked like this:

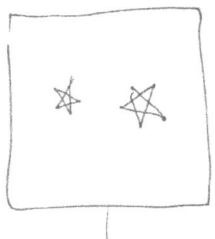

I pointed to that little tail at the bottom of the figure and turned to the class, holding out the chalk. A few hands were tentatively waved and I offered the chalk to one of the wavers. The boy came up and carefully wrote a "2" below the diagram.

That got us started. I drew similar diagrams with different shapes and the children quickly caught on, competing to write the numbers below the figures. Then I began to complicate the requests by erasing their numbers and connecting two figures like this:

No problem. A volunteer wrote "5" below the boxes.

I continued in this fashion, soon replacing the boxes with numbers but using the same connecting segments. All of the children were eagerly participating, but not one word was said by me or by any of them. The only noise in the room was that kind of "ugh, ugh" that the excited students made as they raised their hands to volunteer.

After twenty minutes of this activity, I finally spoke up, calling the children's attention to the fact that none of us had spoken until then. And I turned to their teacher to congratulate them on what we had accomplished.

Unfortunately, my lesson proved nothing to this young woman. Her response was: "Yes, after you left yesterday I really scolded them for their behavior and you saw the result this morning."

Even with the best of efforts, you cannot always win.

I don't want my basic point to be missed here. I have used mathematical examples, but the idea applies to all subject areas: you will be well served if you have some demonstration lessons that you can fit into unusual settings.

Where Do You Find Such Activities?

You find lessons like these that require no background and yet are suitable to given age groups in a variety of sources. I found mine from four sources: my reading of journals and books about teaching, my own experiences as a student in well-taught classrooms, my observation of lessons taught by others and my attendance at both formal and informal meetings of teachers.

Many such activities come from your reading. Journals related to your teaching field describe topics and lessons that you can both enjoy and share with others. This may at first seem like stealing, but every writer I know would be delighted to know that his or her lesson was being duplicated.

Conferences devoted to your teaching subject provide a rich source of such activities. Think about it. Scores of classroom teachers will be presenting their very best lessons. With careful selection of those presenters you can come away with a half-dozen or more activities that you can modify not only for your regular classroom teaching but also for the kind of unusual settings I have illustrated in this chapter.

And at some point you will find that you too can offer such lessons to your teaching community. Once you have developed a bag of tricks, you can share yours with others as well as use them in those unexpected settings.

In doing so you will be well representing your profession.

Letter Twenty-three: Your Personal Reading

> *It is what you read*
> *when you don't have to*
> *that determines*
> *what you will be*
> *when you can't help it.*
> —Oscar Wilde

It is never too early to begin amassing a library of books related to your teaching. But gathering books is only part of my recommendation. Books on a shelf may serve only a decorative role. Think in this regard of those shelves of books you find in lawyers' offices. Today they serve little purpose as almost all of the information they convey is more easily accessed with computers. Now the books themselves have mostly symbolic value: they impress clients or occasionally when one of them is flourished by an attorney in a courtroom a judge and jury.

Of course, your books can serve occasionally as reference — certainly not a bad use — but you will do yourself a service if you also read those books for pleasure and only indirectly as a personal in-service course.

Unfortunately, today our college courses focus tightly on specific content and our education courses focus on pedagogical literature and general teaching methods. Unless you have explored on your own, you have almost certainly not met the classics related to your teaching field.

I recommend that you read for pleasure and not as a task. And the books don't have to have a tight focus on the classroom. What you are really doing is expanding your general background and specific application to your classrooms need only be incidental. In this regard I think of Gradgrind in Dickens' *Hard Times* for English teachers. Gradgrind represents the very worst kind of teacher — and human being for that matter — but he is an often-referenced figure in education and knowing about him contributes to the background of any English teacher. But you don't have to turn to the masters. Best sellers work as well: I think, for example, of Bell Kaufman's *Up the Down Staircase*. No science teacher should fail to read Charles Darwin's wonderful world cruise, *Voyage of the Beagle*, which, for those few who question evolution, has nothing to do with that concept. And some books cross lines: among them Grant's *Memoirs*, his remarkable account of his role in our Civil War that should serve English teachers as literature at the same time it does history teachers as background. I cannot leave this topic without recommending C. P. Snow's Rede lecture, "The Two Cultures," about the chasm that unfortunately exists between the sciences and the humanities.

Those represent only examples of the kind of books that I think would serve your continuing intellectual growth. Such books take you beyond the journal articles of your field that help you to keep up with what is current and immediately useful.

Making Connections

I have suggested reading as motivated by personal enjoyment and self-improvement, but you should be alert to possible classroom uses of what you read. Many times you will come across passages or examples that can be tied into your instructional program. You can add them to your file of useful applications.

I offer here one example of this. In today's school

geometry courses few students have any idea of the history of their course. A major part of what they are studying is an adaptation of Euclid's first of the thirteen books in his *Elements* written 2300 years ago. An exploration of that text in translation is well worth the time of any math teacher.

Your School Librarian

In my experience I have found school librarians to be very supportive and pleased to receive book recommendations. They operate under budgetary limitations and may have to turn down some requests, but you'll gain their respect — and usually the books you seek — if you ask for them. On the other hand, you'll get nothing if you don't ask.

Letter Twenty-four: Professional Activities

> *All I do, really, is go to work*
> *and try to be professional,*
> *be on time and be prepared.*
> — actor Ben Affleck

I continue to counsel you to focus first and foremost on your classroom teaching. Consider that role first, second, third, right down the line. But there are other aspects of your life and your longer-range career that you should begin to think about even during your first year on the job. They can involve you more deeply in your profession.

The teachers in many states are required as part of their teaching contract to belong to teacher unions, either the American Federation of Teachers or the National Education Association. This may come as a shock to some of you with a libertarian bent, but it is simply a fact of your professional life. I urge you to think of these unions in three ways:

1. Especially as a beginner, you have little power within your system. A union is organized to provide you with representation, someone on your side in dealing with your school administration and the public.[51] As a beginning, non-

---

[51] I was a teacher before teachers organized and, although I have some reservations about unions — who doesn't? — I much prefer them to what went before. You would be embarrassed as I was when I began teaching if you read much of what was written then in educational journals. Just as were the schools of those times, they were controlled by the all-powerful school superintendents, who could walk into your classroom and discharge you if they didn't like the color of your necktie.

tenured teacher, I suggest that you not yet become involved deeply in union matters. Stay focused on your teaching and let your seniors represent you.

2. In your teaching do not restrict what you wish to do with and for your students through reference to contract specifics. If, for example, your school day runs from 8:30 a.m. to 4:00 p.m., do not feel that you must not open your classroom door until 8:30 and you must close it at 4:00. You may work with teachers who operate that way, but I urge you to consider your employment as a profession, not a job.

3. Work with your supervisors and administrators on almost all school-related issues. Think long and hard before you seek help from your union representative. If, however, you find yourself facing a serious problem you cannot handle otherwise, do not hesitate to seek help from this person. That is what they are there for. Hopefully this will not happen but, if and when it does, you will appreciate their support.

    Consider, for example, the story I told earlier about inadvertently pushing a student, causing him to fall. In today's super-sensitive school environment that episode might well turn into a legal case of violence toward a defenseless student. You would then find that the union whose dues made you grumble would suddenly become a very positive force in your defense.

Now what about the organizations of your subject field and of general education as well?

You Can't Join Every Organization

You will find that you can invest a substantial part of your salary in memberships. Today there are organizations representing every subject teaching field not only nationally (and internationally) but in your state and sometimes your local area as well. They have names like the National Science Teachers Association, the National Association of the Teachers of English, the North Carolina Association of Elementary

Educators and and the Colorado Council of Teachers of Mathematics. There are also societies for gifted and exceptional students as well as curricular, psychological, historical and sociological organizations. There are enough, quite simply, to make your head whirl.

There are values that attain to each of these organizations. Most sponsor journals, most offer annual system-wide meetings and some sectional meetings as well, and all have committees that address particular aspects of their general concerns. But for fiscal reasons alone you will have to pick and choose.

Admittedly you have plenty to do keeping up with planning your classes and grading tests and homework. Despite this, I urge you to find collegiality with others in your profession through participation. In one school a group of us got together to share journals, each of us joining a different organization. Then we met regularly to report on articles we thought would be of general interest.

If you accept my plea, where should you begin? I suggest with your state organization of teachers of your subject. And don't just join, seek support from your school administration or possibly your union to attend their regional or state-wide meetings.

When you do attend these meetings, even if you simply sit in on a few sessions and look at the book exhibits, you will gain through this break from your day-to-day classroom teaching. You'll feel a greater sense of participation in your profession.

But go out of your way to meet people at these meetings. Join in discussions after sessions. Learn about those seated with you at meals. Talk with textbook representatives: if you show interest in their books, they will often invite you to their company parties. Introduce yourself to speakers whose talks you enjoyed and to officers of the organization. If you see a committee doing something you consider interesting, ask about how you might participate. With a role to play in an organization, you will find it easier to gain support to attend their sessions.

I was fortunate when I was a beginner to have other teachers in my school active in our state organization and they helped me to get through this breaking in period. My university advisor also helped.

Back to School

You may face further education requirements, you may simply wish to gain an advanced degree, or — even simpler — you may wish to extend your education by sitting in on advanced courses. Any of these motivations should take you back to school.

You will need to obtain technical advice from an advisor about how coursework might fit into a program and a good advisor can be very important. My advice: look around, talk to other teachers about their experience with advisors at various nearby colleges. You might even visit more than one before deciding on what school to attend and what direction to take.

And then, I don't need to tell you, choose wisely among the offerings available. In particular, a good instructor can make a poor course come alive while a poor instructor can kill the best.

One thing about course work to which you should be sensitive. Graduate school teachers like all university faculty are concerned with research. It is a significant part of their assignment. You may in time work with those faculty members on research projects, but those should be treated as a completely separate world from your school teaching assignment. Just as I pointed out about my own textbook writing as a diversion from my teaching assignment, so too are research activities. In fact, I consider it not unreasonable to consider many of the projects in which those college teachers are involved antithetical to teaching.

*

In the end, however, you are well advised as a beginning teacher not to overextend yourself. Do not take on too many responsibilities in addition to your classroom assignments. Teaching is a high energy task and you should conserve your resources to perform it successfully.

Letter Twenty-five: The Possibility of Failure

Every adversity, every failure, every heartache,
carries with it the seed
of an equal or greater benefit.
–Napoleon Hill

No beginning teacher wants even to consider the prospect of professional failure. But just as students fail, teachers fail. Some have claimed that less than half survive the first five years of teaching. The data clearly indicate that claim to be overblown, however.[52] In any case, whatever the data, some teachers do not make it and I address that prospect in this letter.

There are many reasons why teachers fail. One is that some of them are placed in impossible settings. A professional circus lion tamer with a chair and a whip would have a difficult time dealing with a particular group of screaming maniacs, yet school administrators glibly assign rank beginners to teach such groups, caring too little about the inevitable results. They often even exacerbate the problem by providing little or no support for this teacher. The blame for those results is then assigned to the beginner.

---

[52] Craig McBride has studied this claim — 12% annual turnover leading to only $(.88)^5 = 53\%$ remaining after five years — and found it to be unsubstantiated when applied to beginners only. Taken from U.S. Department of Labor and Department of Education statistics, this one-half leaving includes all teachers and includes such reasons for leaving as retirement, transfer and role changing such as teachers becoming guidance counselors or administrators.

You have probably seen motion pictures about teachers placed in extremely difficult settings, but who have come through with flying colors. The list of such films is very long:

Blackboard Jungle, To Sir With Love, Up the Down Staircase, Freedom Writers, Conrack, Dead Poets Society, and *Mr. Holland's Opus* come to mind.[53] While I enjoy such films as entertainment, I always find myself thinking about my former teaching colleagues who worked hard to deal with students not half as tough as those in the movie but failed.[54]

This problem of teaching in impossible settings is made worse by today's insistence on evaluating teachers by technology: how well their students do on standardized tests. I am reminded in this regard of a beginning teacher who was assigned 47 students in her homeroom, which contained only 30 desks. "I'll have students hanging out the windows," she complained to her principal. "Don't worry," the principal responded, "you'll have plenty of room." And indeed she did: on no day did more than 15 to 20 students show up. "And

---

[53] I have not included *Stand and Deliver*, because it is a film of a teacher, Jaime Escalante, who *has really* achieved success in a difficult setting. In this sense he and this film represent a counterexample to my list.

[54] The script for these films is boilerplate. Scene One: An impossible situation is established: a school in a dreary urban setting with a blacktop schoolyard strewn with trash, locked school doors and boarded up windows, school halls filled with students screaming, pushing and grappling, a filthy classroom that would better serve Dickens' Wackford Squeers into which several dozen of these half-dressed teenagers (best played by down-on-their-luck actors in their late twenties) arrive to arrange themselves around but not in desks. Scene Two: Enter the young man or woman who will teach these malcontents. And suddenly all is well. The students not only take their seats but the boys shave and both boys and girls adopt reasonable clothing.

My favorite among films of this genre is *Up the Down Staircase*, derived from a humorous novel by Bel Kaufman. I enjoyed the book, but the teacher in the film is acted by Sandy Dennis, an actress with a high whiney voice who is at her best playing roles in which she is bullied. I found myself laughing at the stupidity of the film producers who assigned her this lion-taming role.

some of them lasted only until the free lunch each day," she told me. Despite this, the teachers in that school would be evaluated on all 47 of those students, never mind whether they ever had a chance to teach them.

But even when the setting is reasonable and you have teachable students, you may fail. One very common reason for failure is a difference in philosophy. Many of you have graduated from programs that focus on such things as the development of student creativity and general problem solving skills and now you find yourself in a school whose entire focus is on drill-and-practice. You may be issued a textbook that reflects this approach: each textbook example is followed by dozens of exercises similar to that example, some of them starred, which means that they appeared on past standardized tests. If you don't accommodate to this approach, you can be in trouble. (See Ray Patenaude's response to this kind of situation in Letter Twelve.) You must realize that it is quite possible to be right in your philosophy of teacher education and even a breath of fresh air to your students, yet fail to retain your job.

Early Failures

Far too many beginning teachers fail the first minute they step foot in their classroom. Despite the best of intentions they simply do not fit in this setting. As contemporary headlines too often illustrate, too many teenagers are bullies. Often they adopt this posture as a defense: second-raters themselves, they join in picking on any student or teacher who is different from them in some way — for example, in academic accomplishment — and they seek ways to make that individual uncomfortable.

Accustomed to a culture of achievement, some teachers are unable to accommodate to the culture of their students. When I talk to such teachers, I usually ask them to think back to their own experience in school. The answer they give is either that they attended a school whose focus was on academics or they were isolated and often bullied in a more comprehensive school. While the latter group has a better chance to find a way to fit in, they may carry with them the same characteristics that caused them to be bullied as students.

I always found it easy to pick such prospective teachers out from my college classrooms and I tried to counsel them privately to understand their shortcomings and to think carefully about how to proceed. In most cases these young men and women found it easy to find teaching positions, but few of them succeeded. What bothered me about their failure was the inability of those who hired them to identify the characteristics that were so clear to me. and either not to hire them or to provide them the counseling they would need to survive in the classroom.

A few of those teachers did make it, however; some of them even became very successful in their careers. But almost all of those who did well, taught in settings that accommodated to them rather than the reverse. Most often they taught in private or parochial schools in which academic achievement matched their own preferences. There they found students who shared many of their own characteristics and they were able to manage them satisfactorily.

How Can You Handle Failure?

Okay, let's assume you have failed. You learn that you are no longer to continue in your current position. For most of us this is a devastating experience. It is one thing to fail a course in school or college; it is quite something else to fail at our chosen profession. And often those who fail in a school setting have never experienced failure before: in fact they have usually been exceptionally successful students themselves.

Failing forces you to reassess your future. Should you try to find another teaching position or should you give up on teaching and identify another career?

Before you make that important decision, you should evaluate what went wrong. And here you should not focus on the school setting; rather, you should focus on your own response to that setting. It is too easy to say: the kids were bad, the administration was no help, your colleagues looked only to their own interests and shared nothing with you, the parents interfered, the school was concerned only with successful athletic teams. Every one of those things may be true, but other teachers were able to address those problems and you were not.

I suggest that you take this assignment seriously. Write out a list of the things you did wrong and try to be as specific as possible. It is no help to say you didn't accommodate to your students. It is a rare teacher who does entirely. Remind yourself how you mishandled interactions with individual students, specific events that went wrong, colleagues you irritated. This is a difficult and painful task but, if you take it seriously, it can serve you well.

Once you have made your list, look at each point and rethink it. Could you have done something different and addressed that problem satisfactorily? If you find that you have enough positive answers to those questions, you have every right to decide to try to continue teaching. If not, hopefully then you will have satisfied yourself that teaching is not for you.

Can You Start Over?

Let's assume that your inventory encourages you. Can you find another job? Of course, this depends on the current availability of teaching positions and you have a serious blemish on your record. You will certainly not be dealing from a position of strength.

Here is a suggestion about what you might do. Make an

appointment with the administrator who fired you. At the outset assure your administrator that you are not questioning the decision to let you go. Then share your list of the problems you failed to address satisfactorily and how you believe you can address them. And finally ask for a recommendation that indicates how you are addressing your shortcomings. Such a recommendation can do much to counter the black mark your failure represents.

Starting Over

Be assured that many teachers have failed and then overcome failure. But, if you do find a new position, see to it that you commit as few of your prior errors as possible. This book should be as meaningful to you then as I hope it was when you began your first assignment.

High school teacher Jon Unger offered the following remarks in a 2015 commencement speech at his Madieira High School commencement. Although his suggestions were aimed at graduating seniors, I believe they should speak to you as well:

> As you move into your futures, I am not going to wish you a fairy-tale life where you live happily ever after. I am not going to wish you a road without bumps and dead ends and obstacles. I am not going to wish you a world without hardship. Instead, I am going to wish you the strength to persevere when everything around you is falling apart. I am going to wish you the ability to rise from the ashes and bounce back stronger than ever when it seems like nothing is going your way. I am going to wish you the faith, wisdom, and guidance to overcome all which comes to you, to find the silver lining in every cloud, to find the compensation in every loss. Vince Lombardi, the famous football coach, put it well when he said: 'The glory is not in never falling down. The glory is in

fighting to get up every time you do get knocked down.' Another writer said this thought in a different way which I have always found inspiring: 'Only when the sky is darkest can I see the stars.'[55,56]

---

[55] The closing quotation is a minor revision of a statement by Ralph Waldo Emerson.
[56] Jon Unger's complete commencement talk is posted as of this writing at http://dianeravitch.net/2015/06/08/a-graduate-of-harvard-law-school-whobecame-an-algebra-teacher-addresses-the-class-of-2015/. I recommend it to you as it carries a message to every one of us about commitment and compensation.

ON YOUR WAY

Letter Twenty-six: Ready, Set Go!

> *Your first year of teaching, especially the first few months,*
> *will be a kind of initiation with you on the goat.*
> *The sensation may not be altogether pleasant*
> *but any teacher full of life and eager to go*
> *should get a delightful thrill both from the anticipation*
> *and the achievement of victory.*
> —George Miller

You are embarking on one of the most important jobs in all society: preparing youngsters for the world they will face once they leave school. I honor you for undertaking this task as should anyone who thinks deeply about our society. Your contribution may be a small one but it is important nonetheless.

Your students are not going to approach your desk after class to tell you how much they appreciate what you are doing for them. They simply don't think in those terms. But, if you do well, their appreciation will come over time and, if you are as lucky as I have been, you will receive their feedback in widely scattered episodes.

Let me place this in personal terms. I have received a half dozen awards for college teaching; when I am in academic garb at graduation ceremonies my three medals clank together. But those were easy: as you should have observed by now, the competition is not all that great. Much college teaching is pedestrian.

I appreciate far more the rewarding comments I have accumulated over the years from former high school students: "Yours was my favorite class," "Do you remember when you...," "Believe it or not, you made me enjoy coming to school," and even one student's "I didn't learn much from you but you always made me laugh."

Some are far more serious and each one repays me for all those hours correcting papers. "You made me appreciate how math works." "I became a math teacher because of you." "As you can see, your encouragement has paid off," this from a woman who earns more in a week today than I earned in the year she was my student. And even the occasional, "You turned my life around."

The most unexpected response came from a young woman who struggled to keep up with my advanced class to which she had been assigned. I considered her one of my weakest students. Her parents were going through a hostile divorce and before the year was over she moved away to live with her father. Years later I received a letter from this student. In it she said that my class had carried her through those difficult times, that she often tutored her college classmates using what I had taught her. With the letter she included a paper she had written that had been published in a major mathematical journal. Clearly I had completely underestimated this young woman's abilities and yet I had gained this unexpected accolade.

What is important for you to understand is the fact that my experience is *not unusual*. Experienced teachers all have stories like mine, stories that reinforce us over time. If you do your job well, you can expect the same. And it is important to note that many of my student responses came from young men and women I taught that very first year. There is a kind of freshness and naiveté you bring to your task in your inaugural year that you will never be able to replicate.

I end these letters with a response Betty Krist, one of the two or three finest classroom teachers I know, provided when I asked her for suggestions about this book.[57] "Here," she said, "is my final sermonette to my methods students," and she gave me a perfect mix of the mundane and high-minded that I think perfectly concludes these letters:

Get yourself at least one pair of super-comfortable, QUIET shoes.

Get a hobby or some fun thing to do apart from teaching as boring people make boring teachers.

Have a life. While it's good to be dedicated, you cannot change the world as fast as you'd like and you need to think about how you plan to do this job for the next 30 years or so. Thus you need to regularly get a good night's sleep, eat healthy, enjoy your family and friends.

Learn to speak correctly. Grammar is important.

If you do so, ALWAYS express your extreme displeasure with current circumstances, especially politics, in a polite and disarming fashion.

Drop that pile of papers at the end of a hot and busy day. If you're exasperated, wanting to shout a possibly unacceptable remark, instead have a personal phrase, "Oh dear me" or some other humdrum expression, that is your go-to comment — one that is so inane that it makes you smile and all those around you smile as well. A good time to practice this phrase is in traffic when an irritating driver cuts in front of you.

I guarantee the day will come when you've spent hours on a lesson that was ruined for whatever reason and NO ONE appreciates your talent or effort. Live with it.

---

[57] A photo of Dr. Krist teaching one of the University at Buffalo Gifted Math Program classes enhances the cover of this book. She and I established this program and for many years we co-directed it, Betty taking over full responsibility when I retired.

Buy ONLY washable clothes.

Develop your own teaching style that you EXPECT to evolve.

Keep notes about what you think made a lesson "work". These notes will help your planning next year, but resist the temptation ever to repeat lessons verbatim.

Have fun. Enjoy the math and the kids. Laugh and smile with them. The job's too hard if you're not enjoying yourself and them.

I wish you the very best of luck. As my own high school football coach used to say before every game, "Get in there and give 'em hell."

And remember: the whole world is counting on you.

APPENDIX

Appendix. My Qualifications for this Task

> *A man is like a fraction*
> *whose numerator is what he is*
> *and whose denominator*
> *is what he thinks of himself.*
> *The larger the denominator,*
> *the smaller the fraction.*
> —Leo Tolstoy

Because I offer very personal advice in these letters, I should justify my having done so. Quite simply, I bring many years of experience to this task. In the letters that I offer I draw upon that experience; here I outline it briefly.

When I returned from my three and a half years of naval service during World War II, I still had a semester to complete my undergraduate program at the University of Rochester. During that semester I took mostly evening classes and during the day worked as trainer for the football team of East High School in Rochester. I also served as a substitute teacher in western New York schools. A returning veteran at a time of teacher shortage, my usual certification requirements were bypassed. In one of those schools I taught in an annex to an old building which had its own coal furnace in the back of the room. It made those three months seem like teaching in the old one-room schools you read about in novels.

I also spent a year in graduate school at the university studying English literature. During that year I taught English for a month in that same East High School, where my friends from the football team made accommodating to the school easy for me. I recall assigning three very attractive young women roles as the three witches in MacBeth.

Upon graduation I began my career as a math teacher in New York. I taught successively in rural Warsaw Central High School, in urban Johnson City High School, and in Brighton High School, the suburban school outside Rochester from which I had graduated less than ten years earlier.

I then moved to another Rochester suburb as the Greece Olympia High School mathematics department head, both developing and teaching the math program for that new district secondary school. During those Rochester years I also taught undergraduate mathematics courses for the University of Rochester evening division.

Those represent all of my regular school classroom experience: the familiar five classes, three or four preparations, homeroom, lunchroom duty, class and extracurricular advisement and coaching regimen so familiar to hard-pressed young teachers. (I often tell friends about the 23-game winning streak of the Brighton football team I coached, but I keep quiet about the many losses that we suffered before and after.)

Just thirteen years, not much out of my years of professional experience, I agree, but those were formative years and my subsequent activities have given me plenty of opportunity to reconsider them and to place them in perspective.

My next position was K-14 mathematics coordinator for the City of Norwalk, Connecticut, a school system that included twenty-one elementary schools, four junior high schools, two high schools and a community college. During that period I also taught mathematics education courses for New York University and the University of Connecticut.

After those rewarding years in New York and New

England I headed west to the University of Minnesota where I was appointed director of the Minnesota National Laboratory, a center for the study of mathematics teaching, and assistant director of a "New Math" curriculum development project. While I was there I co-authored with Donovan Johnson, then president of the National Council of Teachers of Mathematics, a textbook for mathematics teacher preparation that was for some years the standard nationwide.

When those government funded programs wound down, I returned to New York State to take a faculty position in the Graduate School of Education at the University at Buffalo. There I not only taught courses for teachers but also mathematics and computer science classes. More important as it applies to these letters, with my colleague, Betty Krist, I established the university's Gifted Math Program for highly qualified regional school students in grades seven through twelve. For over 40 years that program has been one of the most successful school activities for gifted students in the country. Now retired as director, I continue to contribute to the program as an advisor and consultant.

I formally retired from the university as a State University of New York Distinguished Teaching Professor in 1992, but I continue to teach occasional classes and write books related to school mathematics. I also have what I consider my most important contribution to mathematics instruction in press: it is a textbook titled simply *About Mathematics* and it is designed to expose mathematical ideas for those college liberal arts students who so often fear and even hate this subject.

Some related activities over the years: I completed two master's degrees (education, University at Rochester; mathematics, Notre Dame) and a doctorate (mathematics education, New York University) and served a term on the board of directors of the National Council of Teachers of

Mathematics. Less directly related: I also coached track and refereed basketball; served as a camp counselor and director; served as a guide for Canadian canoe trips; taught a Great Books course; worked as a teamster driving a milk truck for two summers; and worked as an engineering assistant on a road construction project. For over twenty years I wrote a weekly natural history column for *The Buffalo News*. Essays largely from those columns have been published in four of my books.

Despite my years of service following my classroom teaching, far more important for these letters were those thirteen years in the classroom surrounded by eager and reluctant, bright and dim, rich and poor, industrious and lazy young men and women.

Literature Cited

> *Only the mediocre are supremely confident of their ability. The better you are, the higher the standards you set yourself – you can see beyond your immediate reach.* —Sir Michael Atiyah

Bauerlein, M. (2013) "The Paradox of Classroom Boredom." *Education Week* **32** (37): 31.

Benezet, L. P. (1935) "The Teaching of Arithmetic I: The Story of an Experiment," *Journal of the National Educational Association* **24** (8): 241-244; II: **24** (9): 301-303 and III: **25** (1): 78.

Boswell, J. (1791) *The Life of Samuel Johnson, LL.D*, edited by C. Hibbert and republished in 1986 by Penguin Classics in New York.

Farley, T. (2009) *Making the Grades: My Misadventures in the Standardized Testing Industry.* San Francisco, CA, BerrettKoehler.

Garelick, Barry (2013) "Problem Solving: Moving from Routine to Nonroutine and Beyond," *Notices of the American Mathematical Society* 60 (10): 1340-1342.

Gladwell, Malcolm (2008) *Outliers: The Story of Success.* New York, Little, Brown and Company.

Grevholm, B. (2003). "Teachers' work in the mathematics classroom and their education. What is the connection?" In C. Bergsten & B. Grevholm, eds., *Challenges in mathematics education. Proceedings from Madif3, 2002*, pp. 96-106. Linköping: SMDFs skriftserie.

Hersh, R. and V. John-Steiner (2011). *Loving + Hating Mathematics: Challenging the Myths of Mathematical Life.*

Princeton, NJ, Princeton University Press.
Hoffman, B. (2003) *The Tyranny of Testing*. Mineola, NY, Dover.
Iversen, J. (2006) *High School Confidential: Secrets of an Undercover Student*. New York, Atria Books.
Kozol, J. (1967) *Death at an Early Age: The Destruction of the Hearts and Minds of Negro Children in the Boston Public Schools*. Boston, MA, Houghton Mifflin.
Kozol, J. (2007) *Letters to a Young Teacher*. New York, Crown.
McBride, Craig (2012) *Components of effective teacher induction programs and the impact of experienced mentors*. (Doctoral dissertation) Retrieved from www.library.uark.edu (UMI 35-02555)
Miller, G. F. (1931). *Letters from a Hard-Boiled Teacher to His Half-Baked Son*. Washington, D.C., Daylio.
Miller, G. F. (1934). *Letters to Principal Patterson*. Washington, D.C., Daylion.
Nasar, S. (1998) *A Beautiful Mind: A Biography of John Forbes Nash, Jr*. New York, NY, Simon & Schuster.
Nichols, S. L. and D. C. Berliner (2007) *Collateral Damage: How High-Stakes Testing Corrupts America's Schools*. Cambridge, MA, Harvard Education.
Popham, W. J. (2001) *The Truth about Testing: An Educator's Call to Action*. Alexandria, VA, Association for Supervision and Curriculum Development.
Ravitch, D. (2011) *The Life and Death of the Great American School System: How Testing and Choice Are Undermining Education*. New York, NY, Basic Books.
Rowlett, P. J. (2013). "Developing a Healthy Scepticism about Technology in Mathematics Teaching." *Journal of Humanistic Mathematics* 3(1): 136-148.
Shiver, J. M. (2010). *Teachers' Beliefs about Mathematics and the Teaching of Mathematics as They Enter the Teaching Profession*. Athens, Georgia, University of Georgia. Ph.D. thesis: 127.
Silverman, D. L. (1971) *Your Move*. New York, NY, McGraw-

Hill.

Staiger, D. O. and J. E. Rockoff (2010). "Searching for Effective Teachers with Imperfect Information." *Journal of Economic Perspectives* **24**(3): 97-118.

Stewart, I. (2006). *Letters to a Young Mathematician*. New York, NY, Basic Books.

Strauser, E. (2009) "The Most Cost Effective Approach to Improve Teacher Education," *Teacher's Net. Gazette* **6** (7).

Wenninger, Magnus J. (1971) *Polyhedron Models*. Cambridge, Cambridge University Press.

Wilson, E. O. (2013). *Letters to a Young Scientist*. New York, NY, Liveright.

www.ingramcontent.com/pod-product-compliance
Lightning Source LLC
Chambersburg PA
CBHW061642040426
42446CB00010B/1545